THE
FINANCIAL
ANXIETY
SOLUTION

THE
FINANCIAL
ANXIETY
SOLUTION

A STEP-BY-STEP WORKBOOK
to stop worrying about money, take control of
your finances, and live a happier life

LINDSAY BRYAN-PODVIN, LMSW

Published in the United States by:
ULYSSES PRESS
P.O. Box 3440
Berkeley, CA 94703
www.ulyssespress.com

ISBN: 978-1-64604-007-0
Library of Congress Control Number: 2019951399

Printed in the United States by Kingery Printing Company
10 9 8 7 6 5 4 3 2 1

Acquisitions editor: Bridget Thoreson
Managing editor: Claire Chun
Editor: Renee Rutledge
Proofreader: Miriam Jones
Cover design: David Hastings
Interior design: Jake Flaherty
Interior art: all art © shutterstock.com; page 25 © AV art; page 102 © solar22; page 103 © jesadaphorn; page 103 © Satika

CONTENTS

CHAPTER 6

CALMING YOUR BODY AND MIND 87

CHAPTER 7

BEING SOCIAL WITH FINANCIAL ANXIETY. 111

CHAPTER 8

LOOKING FORWARD. 123

INTRODUCTION

Financial anxiety is a problem. It consists of negative or avoidant thoughts and feelings about money. This anxiety often leads to behaviors like avoiding the bills, procrastinating on signing up for an employers' retirement plan, or not planning for the financial future. A person with financial anxiety can feel guilty, embarrassed, or fearful of their money. Their heart races when the bill comes at dinner, their stomach drops when they have to talk about their salary at their annual performance review, and they feel demoralized when they don't understand what's going on in their retirement account. They think they aren't smart enough to manage their money or don't have enough of it to matter, or they hold a Pollyanna belief that their money will sort itself out.

These types of emotional and behavioral responses contribute to the fact that 60% of Americans can't scrape up $1,000 in the case of an emergency. Over 51% of Americans agree to feeling anxious; money is ranked second in terms of what is stressing Americans out, with 62% of them saying it is a significant source of stress.

The solution? Learn how to cope with financial anxiety so you can become resilient and create a smart financial plan.

I'm Lindsay. I'm a mental health therapist and have spent years working with clients who have financial stressors. Before becoming a financial therapist, the only thing I was trained to do was to help clients find a temporary solution to a permanent problem. This "solution" (usually helping someone call an 800 number to see if they qualified for a bill payment plan) didn't sit well with me. According to my code of ethics as a social worker, I should move beyond merely serving and problem-solving. I should work alongside a client to explore their ability to address their own needs. I should help them understand what's going on so they can have the right information moving forward to manage their lives autonomously. When it comes to financial stressors, I was determined to find a better way than the status quo of bandaging the problem.

As a personal finance nerd in my own time, it became my mission to educate people on financial issues in an ungimmicky, approachable, and emotionally minded way. My approach has resonated. My practice has been full with a waitlist, which is why it's the optimal time for me to share the exact exercises I do with my private financial therapy clients through this book.

Anxiety is treatable. Financial literacy is possible. No matter what our style of learning, most of us do best when we can see a concept put into action. That's why *The Financial Anxiety Solution* is full of examples and scenarios in addition to helpful, usable worksheets. I will walk you step by step through various exercises and strategies to understand your anxiety. I will teach you how to apply coping skills to your anxiety symptoms so you can be in a better place to tackle your financial worries. While this workbook does include financial terms, I will explain each one clearly and without patronizing.

Anyone can google their way to a budget spreadsheet; my goal is to help you figure out why anxiety is getting you caught in financial ruminations, procrastination, or avoidance. Techniques I provide include positive coping skills, quizzes, journaling prompts, calming the mind and body, increasing knowledge about financial terms, and tuning into personal values. I include real-life examples from myself, my friends, and clients (note: any identifying factors have been changed for privacy). When you are ready to see how learning these skills might apply to your finances, I've included shortened versions of some of the most popular money-management techniques.

So what will you get, exactly, from this workbook? The power to be in control of your financial anxiety so you can confidently manage your money. You'll stop dodging your monthly expenses. You'll start calmly and deeply breathing when you plan your financial future. You'll know that your net worth doesn't equal your self-worth.

While I believe most people can benefit from this workbook, it is not for you if you are seeking personalized financial or investment advice, are extremely financially strained, or are seeking a get-rich-quick solution to your financial anxiety. It's not for you if you aren't interested in learning the "whys" behind your financial behaviors.

This workbook is for you if who are ready and willing to get unstuck from your current anxious relationship with your finances. It is for you if you know you are capable of understanding your financial anxiety and are eager to learn steps to alleviate it. This workbook is especially useful if you are in the workforce or about to enter the workforce. While retirees can undoubtedly benefit from the emotional exercises, they may find some of the worksheets no longer apply to their circumstances. This workbook is also a better fit for those who are not in dire financial situations. For example, you may be struggling to make ends meet, but you aren't on the brink of homelessness or bankruptcy.

As the Chinese proverb goes, "The best time to plant a tree was twenty years ago. The second-best time is now." In other words, even if you feel like you are too far into your financial relationship to make a change, there is still hope and opportunity for growth.

I promise that if you take this workbook seriously and dedicate time and energy to it, you'll finish feeling more abundant and less anxious in your relationship with money. You'll log into your bank accounts with a sense of confidence. You'll smile as you think ahead to your realistic five- and ten-year financial goals. You'll pay your bills on time with ease. You'll know how to set yourself up for financial success.

One more note before you get started. You can skim this workbook. You can read the exercises and skip over them. If you skim and skip, I can guarantee you that this workbook won't be useful. For you to truly make a change, you are going to have to commit to reading, processing, and writing. This workbook is designed to build on lessons and techniques from the previous chapters. I encourage you to go through this workbook, in order, from start to finish for the best results.

Remind yourself what is on the other side of financial anxiety.

Let's dive in.

CHAPTER 1

GETTING STARTED

Money isn't a dirty word. You can create a healthy, unanxious relationship with money.

MY MONEY STORY

Our money stories start to take shape when we are quite young. Like many of our beliefs, they form not only from what we learn firsthand but also from what we absorb from the stories our parents and grandparents tell us, the communities in which we live, and the lessons we learn from our education and cultural systems.

My life growing up was drastically different from my maternal grandfather's. He grew up in extreme poverty in rural Texas and Arizona. His parents struggled with mental illness and difficulty holding and maintaining jobs. He used a nail to hold up his overalls when the clasp broke. In his early adolescence, he ran away from home, found respite in a Boy Scout camp, and lied on a job application about his age so he could start working at a restaurant before he was legally able. He applied for and got scholarships for both undergraduate and graduate school to study education and sociology. He moved his six children across the US to follow job opportunities. His money story and the beliefs he freely shared were along the lines of, "Investing in education is the smartest thing you can do for your money and your mind," and "Make sure you always have money set aside because you never know what life will throw at you."

I, on the other hand, grew up in a very financially stable home, where bills were paid in full and on time. My parents spent money on additional tutoring if my sisters and I needed it. We took a vacation annually. My dad shopped almost exclusively at Costco and Big Lots. My mom kept her cars for at least eight years and 200K miles. They always reminded my sisters and me of how fortunate we were and how different our lives were from many. My parents taught me the value of saving and spending in line with their values.

Growing up privileged also meant that I struggled with things like, "Why do we have this lifestyle when so many others don't?" and "Are people going to think I'm an asshole because I come from money?" There were times when I tried on other personas for size, to avoid being pigeonholed into the poor-little-rich-girl box. Those types of anxious thoughts and worries could have easily manifested themselves into unhealthy financial anxiety. I could have ended up deciding that having money made me bad, and stayed at the first nonprofit I worked at, where I made less money than I did as a waitress in college.

In my early twenties, I was in recovery from an eating disorder. And it was around that time that I started to dive into the world of personal finance. At first, I was drinking the restriction and shame Kool-Aid that is ripe in the world of personal finance. It sounded like, "Cut lattes! Remove Uber from your phone! You are stupid if you have debt!" I could see how restricting my spending would create a climate ripe for bingeing, shame, and secrets. It felt way too familiar and terrifying. And I couldn't let that happen.

That's why I preach financial empowerment. That's why I don't let money become something shameful, gross, or taboo. That's why I tell all of my clients that they can cut spending if they want, but the real path to financial stability is increasing their income and feeling amazing about the money they currently have. That's why I encourage you, my dear reader, to have f*cking FUN with their money.

By applying the coping skills I'm about to teach you, I've adapted a healthy, empowered money story that sounds like: "I believe that if you are born into a life of privilege, you should give back to your community," "Money is a tool that can provide peace of mind, and happiness," and "Money isn't the only thing that is important in life, but having it helps to free up mental energy to spend on other things."

MONEY AND ANXIETY

Most Americans today experience some degree of anxiety. At the time of this writing, over 51% of Americans agree to feeling anxious, and 18% of Americans meet the criteria for an anxiety disorder. Money is ranked number two in terms of what is stressing Americans out, with 62% of them saying it is a significant or somewhat significant source of stress. Financial anxiety results in ineffectively interacting with money. That means making financial decisions quickly, irrationally, or without weighing the pros and cons in order to avoid dealing with finances.

When it comes to dealing with your finances, the more anxious you are, the less likely you will be to take action toward improving your financial health. This unhealthy attitude toward thinking about or engaging with personal finances often looks like the following:

- Physical symptoms such as a racing heart, difficulty breathing, nausea, tingling, sweating, and dizziness.

- Second-guessing after you make a 401(k) index fund selection.

- The pit in your stomach when the bill comes at a dinner with friends.

- Avoidance when your partner wants to talk about household bills.

Financial anxiety isn't recognizable in the *Diagnostic and Statistical Manual of Mental Disorders*, the so-called Bible of mental illnesses, but it is something more financial planners, behavioral economists, and financial therapists are recognizing and caring for, even if it isn't "officially" in the book.

DISTRACTION-FREE ZONE

Money is awkward and uncomfortable for many people. In this workbook, I'll be talking a lot about the way the mind, body, actions, and environment are interconnected. As this topic can be difficult, let's get started by setting up the environment to be as soothing and relaxing as possible. Don't try to dive into this for the first time as you sit on the subway commuting to work. Don't try to scribble down some responses while your kiddo is down for their nap. Don't try to reflect on things while you wait for dinner to finish cooking. As I'd mentioned in the introduction, you'll get out of this book what you put into it. So start by finding a quiet space where you can truly relax and dive in. Put your phone on airplane mode if possible. If that causes too much anxiety, at least turn the ringer off or put your phone on Do Not Disturb mode.

In addition to creating a distraction-free zone, have something available for your other senses. I often offer my clients a calming beverage before getting into financial therapy work. The sense of a warm, ceramic mug in your hand, with the aroma of cinnamon wafting from it can help calm initial nerves. According to folklore (or magic, if you're into that), ginger, cinnamon, thyme, lemon, and chamomile have been associated with wealth and abundance. Whether or not you buy into that is up to you, but either way, it's nice to have something on hand to help set the tone as you set your intentions for the book.

Here are three different beverages you may want to prepare to help you get in the anxiety-free mindset before settling in.

Sparkling Water with Thyme and/or Lemon

Pour yourself a glass of sparkling water and garnish with a sprig of thyme and a wedge of lemon.

Abundance Cocktail/Basil Ginger Gimlet

4 basil leaves

½ to 1 small lime, juiced

ice

1.5 ounces gin (optional)

3 ounces ginger ale or ginger beer

In the bottom of a glass, muddle the basil leaves until they begin to wilt. Squeeze ½ of the lime juice into the glass, adding more to taste. Add ice and gin (if using) and stir together. Top with ginger ale or ginger beer.

Money Tea

Using your favorite style of loose-leaf or bagged tea, steep a cup of cinnamon or chamomile tea.

Now that you have your beverage on hand, let's get started. I'm all about shifting your mindset to better work for you. I don't believe in vision-boarding or manifesting without taking action-able steps.

SETTING INTENTIONS

Let's first define what a mindset is. Mindset is simply your frame of mind that shapes the way in which you see and interpret things in the world. A mindset that certain things are fixed will frame the way you view yourself and others. Let's say a person identifies with the personality trait of being stubborn. They are attached to the mindset that being stubborn is a fixed trait, and something that they have to deal with and others need to learn how to handle. This could set up this person to sell themselves short when it comes to being flexible or open-minded.

"Well, I'm just stubborn. That's the way I see it, so that's the way it is." If this person had the mindset that stubbornness, while it is a trait, isn't necessarily a fixed one, it could open them up for more possibilities. It could allow them to be open to learning new things, practice being humble, and be more approachable to others' viewpoints. Living with the mindset that stubbornness just "is" closes them off from viewing themselves as a person who is more well-rounded.

When it comes to money mindset, start by looking at what ways your mindset has been shaped over time. What stories have you told yourself about money? What lessons have you learned about wealth? Are these fixed traits, or are there opportunities for change?

Let's say a person has the mindset that money is finite. They believe there is only so much money in the world, and that for each person who gets a raise or a bonus, that means there is less money for others. How might this harm them? It could certainly set them up to feel like the world is unfair. Perhaps as they clap their coworker on the back when they get a promotion, inside they are feeling that their coworker took an opportunity away from them. Let's contrast that with the mindset that money is simply a tool, and that there is plenty of money in the world for everyone. How might this person respond to a coworker's promotion? They might clap their coworker on the back and think to themselves, "I'm so happy for her. That helps me see that it's possible for me to get a promotion, too."

In this chapter, we will start with the intention or mindset as the foundation, then layer on the action steps. Research shows that shifting your mindset to align with your desired outcome is more likely to help you achieve that outcome. Research also shows that writing your goal down makes you 42% more likely to achieve that goal.

• COME UP WITH YOUR INTENTION •

Set a goal or an intention to ensure you are engaging with this workbook for a reason that is yours and yours alone. Examples are provided; feel free to use them directly or draw inspiration from them if they resonate. It's important to either write these in the present or present continuous tense. This seemingly small detail makes a difference. Writing in the present tense sends a subtle shift to your brain that this statement is happening now, in the present moment. Writing in the future tense, as many people tend to do with goal setting, makes that goal seem distant or off in the land of "someday." As in "I will drink more water," versus, "I am drinking more water each day." If the later still feels off, you can try adding "I am working on" or "I am in the process of" before the sentence to make it feel more realistic; as in "I am working on drinking more water each day."

I am looking at my bank account without feeling nauseous.

I understand the importance of putting myself first financially.

I stopped giving or spending my money in ways that don't align with my values.

I recognize the signals my body is sending me as anxiety increases.

I am moving past my financial mistakes and balancing my mind-money relationship.

Your turn. Use the prompts below to see what comes to mind. You may end up with several intentions, or just one that resonates. Whatever the case, use the intention(s) as you work through this book.

I am _____

I understand _____

I am working toward _____

I stopped _____

START FROM THE BEGINNING

With your intention now set, we can work on reflecting on the things that contribute to your current money mindset. I can't tell you how many of my clients come to me prioritizing someone else's needs. Too often, they are confused or frustrated, then when we do the numbers, their money is spent on others first. By others, I also mean other "things." They could be spending money on nights out with neighbors, shopping for their niece's birthday, or upgrading their car lease. In this exercise, I invite you to start with yourself. Yes, this is the "oxygen mask on yourself first" drill. Think about getting yourself in a good space before thinking about how you can help others financially.

• YOUR RELATIONSHIP WITH MONEY •

What do you want your relationship with money to look like? This exercise will help you acknowledge that you do have a relationship with money. This is the basis of setting your new money story or intention. This is the foundation on which the rest of your money story will be built. You can't talk about your spouse's money habits, trying to teach your kids about money, or communicating with your aging parents about their money until you know intimately what your relationship will look like.

What is my relationship with money like?

_____

_____

_____

What is my money doing for me? What do I want my money to do for me?

_____

_____

_____

Do I want it to be the tool that takes care of my basic needs? How can I take back the power over my money?

_____

_____

_____

What is my money doing for others; for my community? Long-term, what do I want my money to do for my community, for charities, for family?

_____

_____

_____

Donating, shopping, or giving to others only comes after you take care of what your money is doing for you, and what your money is doing for your family. Too often, people do these things before getting their own relationship with money figured out. For example, some clients are adamant about giving to their religious institution when they don't yet have an emergency fund (don't worry about an emergency fund yet, we'll get to it later in this book). My belief is that you have to have your personal finance house in order before you can freely give to others. It's not charitable or generous to rob yourself of security.

CHECKING IN WITH YOUR BODY

Our bodies often do an amazing job of signaling us when something is or isn't good for us. You know that pit in your stomach when you walk into work and realize you left your laptop at home on the counter? Yup, that is an example of your body sending you a signal that something is amiss. And while our bodies often tell us what is going wrong, there are plenty of times when they also tell us when things are going right. In order to access this information, you have to get in touch with your body. One of the easiest ways to do so is through a simple grounding exercise. Use this example to practice tuning in to your body. That way, in the future, your body's physical responses can give you insight into your emotional state. You can use the worksheet to get you started, but know that in the future, you don't need to write down your responses. You can do this exercise anywhere at any time.

● SIMPLE GROUNDING EXERCISE ●

Write down what you are experiencing in this very moment. I will build on this exercise later in this book by applying techniques from Martha Beck, PhD, a Harvard-trained sociologist and coach who helps her clients use both cognitive and body-based tools to achieve their goals.

5. *List five things you can see: people, water bottle, phone, pen, lamp*

1._____

2._____

3._____

4._____

5._____

4. *List four things you can feel: hair, jewelry, your feet in your shoes, a book*

1._____

2._____

3._____

4._____

3. *List three things you can hear: footsteps, air conditioner blowing, music*

1._____

2._____

3._____

2. *List two things you can smell: cologne or perfume, lunch*

1._____

2._____

1. *List one thing you can taste:* toothpaste

1._____

This simple exercise does several things. It gets you out of your head temporarily, allows you to pause, and also allows you to check in with how your body is feeling. Additional questions you can add are:

What does my stomach feel like? Hungry, nauseous, knotted up?

_____

Is there any tension in my body? Perhaps my lower back, jaw, or shoulders?

_____

How is my breathing? Relaxed, shallow, forced?

_____

YOUR MONEY STORY

How can you earn money, serve others, and take care of your needs? Money isn't just about the numbers; it's about your relationship with yourself. To shift your relationship with money, you have to reflect on your younger years in a compassionate, blame-free way. Money is a tool we interact with on a daily basis and yet, most of us aren't given the opportunity to learn or talk about it in the way we might with other things. Many of our beliefs around money start when we are children, and some psychologists suggest our money story, or the story or belief we have about money and the way that we view money's role in our world and the world at large, is ingrained by age eight. (According to child development experts,[1] we are able to grasp the concept of death at age seven. What does this mean? It means money is more complex that the idea of death for most of us to comprehend.) A money story is similar to a money mindset. Working toward a balanced, shame-free money story means untangling your younger self from your current reality.

A person's money story could be that money corrupts people. Let's say, for example, Corrine believes money makes people corrupt. Her mom taught her this at a young age and reinforced

---

1   M. W. Speece and S. B. Brent, "Children's Understanding of Death: A Review of Three Components of a Death Concept," *Child Development* 55, no. 5 (1984): 1671–86.

it by pointing out people at church who wore flashy clothes, saying things like, "See them? They think they are better than us because of the things they have on." Corrine goes through life rolling her eyes at those who flash their wealth. She avoids buying name-brand clothes because she thinks it is a waste. She stays late at work even though she isn't paid overtime because it's the right thing to do. She donates to her church, attends community fundraisers, and shops exclusively at thrift stores. She's been in her line of work as an editor for eight years. She has been offered a promotion twice and turned it down both times because "more money doesn't help anybody," and she worried that taking a raise would pull her away from her beliefs that having more money makes you a worse person.

On the other hand, you have Lamar, who has the money story that money would solve all of his problems. He watched his parents struggle financially, and his dad regularly held two to three jobs his entire life. Lamar attended college on a full-ride scholarship and has been working for a few years at a renowned engineering firm. He constantly monitors his bank account, religiously checks the status of his 401(k) investments, and often moonlights as a dog walker on weekends for extra money. While most people would see his life as comfortable, he feels there is never enough money. There are times when he is so anxious that he is messing something up financially that he is unable to hang out with friends.

Don't think you have a money story? Doubtful. As mentioned in the last exercise, we all have a relationship with money, whether or not we think we do. Think about how you are currently telling yourself about money. Are you saying, "I'm terrible at budgeting so I might as well rack up my credit card," or "If I ask for a raise at work, they'll think I'm being greedy." In this exercise, you'll start to formulate the things you tell yourself about money by looking back in time. Bari Tessler, one of the founders of financial therapy, loves talking about the body's connection to our money stories. She often guides her clients or students through similar exercises.

• RECALL A MIND/BODY MONEY STORY •

Call to mind a time when you were younger, under the age of ten. Allow money memories to surface. If a time in your life when you were a bit older than ten is coming up, allow yourself to go there. Maybe there isn't a specific moment, but a series of moments, or a theme that arises. If you are struggling, it could be recalling a time a friend's mom paid for pizza at a sleepover, getting in trouble for taking a candy bar without paying at the corner store, parents sitting around the table paying bills, or a sibling taking your allowance. Perhaps you heard your dad say things like, "Oh, I'm going to hit it big this weekend at the track!" or your mom say things like, "I'll only take you clothes shopping if you outgrow your current ones."

What memories came up?

_____

_____

_____

_____

What thoughts do you have about those memories now?

_____

_____

_____

_____

Was it surprising?

_____

_____

_____

_____

Were any physical sensations prominent for you?

_____

_____

_____

_____

_____

What was the theme around money growing up?

_____

_____

_____

_____

_____

• MONEY STORY JOURNALING •

Perhaps the idea of going back into your younger years to tap into your money story wasn't resonating. Maybe you are more concrete and want to focus on specific moments rather than distant memories or themes about money. If so, take the time to answer the following questions about money. This may help you get a clearer sense of things that shape your money story and consequent money mindset.

Who was in charge of household finances growing up?

_____

What did your parents do to earn a living?

_____

Do you have a rough idea of how much money they made?

_____

What's one of your best memories about money?

_____

_____

_____

What's one of your worst memories about money?

_____

_____

_____

What was your first paid job? How were you paid? Under the table in cash or above board with a paycheck? How much did you make?

_____

_____

_____

MONEY SCRIPT SELF-ASSESSMENT

There are four types of money scripts, according to Dr. Brad Klontz, a financial psychologist.[2] They are Avoider, Worshipper, Vigilance, and Status. The Avoider tends to have a negative association with money, as in "Rich people are greedy," or "It's virtuous to live with less money." Worshippers are the people who believe that happiness is directly tied to more money. Those who are Vigilant are very concerned about their financial health to the point that they may pinch pennies to the detriment of their relationships. The Status-minded are

2   D. Lawson, B. Klontz, and S. L. Britt, "Money Scripts," in *Financial Therapy*, eds. B. Klontz, S. L. Britt, and K. L. Archuleta (New York: Springer, 2015), 23–24.

those who link their self-worth to their net worth. While the Worshipper and Status-minded appear similar, the easy way to differentiate the two is that Worshipers value money whereas the Status-minded value what money buys or represents. Money scripts are the subconscious or unconscious belief about money that are learned in childhood and passed down generationally. These scripts have been found to contribute to a person's financial health, outcomes, and money story.

Olivia Mellan, a psychotherapist and pioneer in the work of money psychology, also has her version of money scripts she sees in her work. She categorizes clients into one of five domains: Hoarder, Spender, Money Monk, Avoider, and Amasser.[3] Hoarders like to save money and have a hard time spending money on themselves or others. Spenders get satisfaction from spending their money, whether it's on themselves or others. Money Monks have a deep belief that money is bad or dirty and feel anxious if they accumulate "too much" of it for fear that they will change into a "bad" person. Avoiders don't look at their money, either due to overwhelm or feeling incompetent. An Amasser is happiest when they have large amounts of money at their disposal to spend, save, or invest, as they equate self-worth with net worth.

While I find these money scripts and types to be a good starting point, I have found groupings in my work that tend to be similar but are more my style, meaning they are less rigid and take time to include the positive side of each of these personas. There's always a silver lining. While these positives aren't outlined in research, I've seen a lot of strengths in my clients. I've seen resilience, dedication, empathy, charity, and strong work ethics. It's important to remember that no one person is going to neatly fit into a category, so when reviewing these money personas, just look for the one that sounds the *most* like you. Once you find out which persona you are most like, it will help guide you moving forward.

• YOUR MONEY PERSONA •

Instructions: Review the four sets of personality types and statements. Choose the one that sounds the most like you to learn more about your money persona.

A: The idea of money and talking about it makes you cringe. You feel it's rude or gauche to talk about it. You may resist talking about money because it is "private." You avoid looking at bank statements, credit card bills, or any money-related paper trail for fear of what you might find. You have no idea if you are investing in or contributing enough for retirement. You're not entirely sure how you don't run out of money each month, but you haven't yet. You're

---

3 O. Mellan, S. Christie, J. Bodnar, and P. McMoon, *Money Harmony: A Road Map for Individuals and Couples* (Washington, DC: Money Harmony Books, 2014).

certain it'll just work out. You feel better not knowing because ignorance is bliss. You find yourself agreeing with statements like, "I do not deserve money when others have less than me. Wanting more than 'just enough' is selfish. Good people should not care about money."

B: You can't stop chasing money. Your side hustle has a side hustle. You feel gross when you have downtime and aren't earning money. You are refreshing Reddit feeds on personal finance to see if there is a new tax break or saving strategy you haven't fully used to your advantage. You are always thinking about how much interest you are earning and what stocks are going to be the next big winners. Every time you hit a financial goal, you immediately set a new milestone before allowing yourself to celebrate a victory. You find yourself agreeing with statements like, "More money will make me happier. Money would solve all of my problems. Money buys freedom."

C: Your savings money goes beyond having a solid emergency fund and retirement account. You have anxiety buying ice cream from the new creamery in your neighborhood because there is perfectly good ice cream at home. You feel yourself start to sweat when a friend asks you to meet them at happy hour to talk about their new job. Your pulse quickens when your partner encourages you to use a gift card you've been carrying in your wallet for over three years. You are terrified of seeing "insufficient funds." You find yourself agreeing with statements like, "You should not tell others how much money you have or make. Money should be saved, not spent. It's irresponsible to not have an emergency fund."

D: Your money is burning a hole in the proverbial pocket. You get a rush out of buying an armful of new hiking gear from REI or loading up your Sephora shopping cart. You find a way to furnish your living room with Restoration Hardware even when it means the couch goes on a credit card. When cash comes into your life, it flows out just as easily. You tend to agree with statements like, "Even when I don't mean to, I trend toward buying name-brand items. If something isn't the best, it isn't worth buying. I get a rush when I swipe my credit card."

Answer:

A = Blissfully Ignorant
Unhelpful thoughts/behaviors: By trending toward the belief that money is for people who are greedy or corrupt, you may self-sabotage when it comes to your financial success. Sometimes this looks like giving money away, other times it means spending too much or not advocating for yourself. You try not to think about money. For example, you may avoid looking at bank statements, talking to a partner about money, or engaging in family financial discussions.

Potential strengths: You tend to give back to your community via volunteering instead of with financial donations. Once in alignment with your money, you have the ability to check in on your money less frequently. Work toward accepting abundance into your life on a monetary level.

B=Money Admirer

Unhelpful thoughts/behaviors: You believe the secret to happiness and the solution to your problems is to have more money. You have a hard time being happy with your current net worth and are often striving for the "next level" due to a false belief that once you have X dollars, then you'll feel better, be happy, experience satisfaction, etc.

Potential Strengths: You don't get anxious looking at your money, so you have an ability to look at your checking account and investment returns objectively. You have a strong work ethic and capacity for entrepreneurship. You're likely to be charitable to family and friends. You understand the desire for money and respect a partner who enjoys working. You can work toward finding value in nonmonetary ways, such as through health, spirituality, and relationships.

C=Doomsday Prepper

Unhelpful thoughts/behaviors: You have a true scarcity mindset when it comes to your money. You believe that money is a finite resource and have a fear-based relationship it. You believe it is important to save and for people to work for their money rather than be given financial handouts. You have a tendency to be somewhat anxious about your financial future and worry that your money will run out or disappear. Excessive wariness or anxiety can prevent you from enjoying the benefits and sense of security that money can provide.

Potential Strengths: You're less likely to buy on credit or to keep financial secrets from your partner. You're good at saving money, planning ahead, and working toward a debt-free life. You can work toward the belief that money can also expand life's opportunities and experiences.

D=Spender

Unhelpful thoughts/behaviors: You are likely to link your self-worth with your net worth. You may prioritize outward displays of wealth, and as a result, can be at risk of overspending. You are also more likely to gamble excessively, be financially dependent on others, and hide expenditures from your spouse. You love spending for yourself and others and rarely attend an event without bringing "a little something" for the host.

Potential Strengths: You have the capacity to work hard for yourself and your family. With a strong capacity for spirituality, you're likely to believe in the power of the universe to take care of your financial needs. You can work toward handling success with grace and humility and are working on being at ease with "good enough."

• MONEY STRENGTHS AND CHALLENGES •

Using what you learned from your money persona assessment, think about your personal challenges and strengths.

My money challenges:

_____

_____

_____

_____

_____

My money strengths:

_____

_____

_____

_____

_____

Now that you have an idea of where your money story started, what you want your money to do for you, and your financial personality, you are ready to move onto the basics of anxiety.

My top three takeaways from this chapter:

1._____

2._____

3._____

CHAPTER 2

ANXIETY

"Breathe. Start where you are, hold yourself and your money past without shame. Create for yourself a 'no shame zone' about the financial past and focus on your financial future."

—Saundra Davis, founder of Sage Financial

Before focusing solely on financial therapy, I spent years as a practicing therapist helping clients with anxiety. In traditional psychotherapy, a large part of the work with clients is providing them with information on their diagnosis and symptoms. This is called psychoeducation. What we know about providing psychoeducation is that it gives a person the feeling of empowerment once they have an understanding of what is or isn't a part of their disorder. In this chapter, I'll go over what anxiety is, when it becomes problematic, and how it shows up physically, mentally, and emotionally. My intention is to help you feel empowered to recognize and quiet your anxiety.

CLINICAL VS. TYPICAL ANXIETY

"When anxiety strikes, its first move is to convince you you're all alone. The first countermove is to remember that you aren't."

—Mollie Fisher, host of *The Cut on Tuesdays*

All humans experience anxiety. Anxiety is a normal, healthy reaction to a stressor. It might look like worry or apprehension. It is part of the fight-flight-freeze response, a protective mechanism that has aided in our survival for millennia. Healthy anxiety is time-limited, meaning it doesn't stay at a heightened alert for an extended period of time. For example, when you are about to give a presentation at work, your heart rate goes up and your throat gets a bit tight, but it fades once you are done presenting. In this book, I am not addressing clinical, chronic anxiety but the everyday, time-limited anxiety. Just because it is time-limited doesn't mean it isn't impactful. When it comes to finances, financial anxiety can lead to avoiding taking financial action and the loss of compound interest (more on that later). It can also manifest in a number of ways. As you go through this chapter, you'll be able to identify how financial anxiety shows up for you and healthy ways for you to address it.

Clinical anxiety, on the other hand, is an overly excessive response to the stressor AND impacts a person's ability to function. This is when anxiety becomes difficult to control. This type of anxiety comes along with an almost-constant feeling of being on edge and difficulty relaxing because you are worrying too much. Clinical anxiety is distressing and gets in the way of a person being able to live their lives fully. For example, when you replay something you've said over and over and it makes you feel physically sick, makes it hard for you to sleep, and takes away your desire to spend time with people, this could be a sign of clinical anxiety. Please note, you cannot diagnose yourself with clinical anxiety. If you are concerned that your anxiety may be tipping from normal into clinical, see your primary care provider for a mental health evaluation and referral.

ANXIETY AND THE BODY

It wasn't uncommon for me to get anxiety clients following a thorough physical workup that had no findings. Meaning, I'd see clients who thought they had food allergies because their stomach was in so much pain. I'd see people who were convinced they had vertigo because of chronic dizziness. I'd see patients following a visit to the ER because they thought they'd had a heart attack. When people say, "It's all in your head," it's dismissive and also undermines the sheer power of the mind-body connection. None of these people who came to me were making up their symptoms. Their anxiety was so severe that it had manifested as mysterious physical ailments.

In Chapter 1, you practiced connecting with your body in a grounding exercise? You are going to be reconnecting to your body again in this chapter. Anxiety shows up in the body in a very physical way. The physiology of stress can present as a racing heart, sweating, stomach pain (like nausea or no appetite), fast, shallow breathing, a tingling sensation in the arms or legs, a lump or tightness in the throat, dry mouth, neck or jaw tension, or head pain. The specific symptoms vary from person to person, but when you know what anxiety feels like for you, you'll be in a better place to identify it. A former client knew they were on the brink of anxiety when they felt their body "turn to lead" and simultaneously felt light-headed.

● FIND YOUR SYMPTOMS ●

Area:_____

Symptoms:_____

_____

_____

Area:_____

Symptoms:_____

_____

_____

Area:_____

Symptoms:_____

_____

_____

Area:_____

Symptoms:_____

_____

_____

Area:_____

Symptoms:_____

_____

_____

Area:_____

Symptoms:_____

_____

_____

Area:_____

Symptoms:_____

_____

_____

Area:_____

Symptoms:_____

_____

_____

Circle the areas of your body you know are impacted by anxiety. On the corresponding lines, write which symptoms you specifically feel in that area.

CALM YOUR MIND

Anxiety isn't just physical; it shows up cognitively as well. Cognitive symptoms of anxiety include difficulty concentrating, difficulty sustaining attention, poor judgment, racing thoughts, and distorted or unrealistic thoughts. In the next exercise, I'll review common cognitive distortions when a person is experiencing heightened anxiety. A cognitive distortion, initially defined by Dr. Aaron Beck, is simply an exaggerated or irrational thought. We all experience cognitive distortions, but they typically increase during times of stress.

• COMMON COGNITIVE DISTORTIONS •

Listed below are common types of cognitive distortions, along with examples of how they might sound. Check the box next to the distortion if you find yourself thinking in that way. On the space following the examples, if applicable, write down your real-life version of a corresponding cognitive distortion.

All-or-Nothing Thinking: Also called black-and-white thinking. This means you are seeing things as 100% one way or another, you have difficulty seeing the nuances or shades of gray in situations. Examples: "I either do it right or not at all," "Since I blew last month's budget, I shouldn't bother trying again," or "It'd be easier to manage my money if I had more of it."

My all-or-nothing thinking:

_____

_____

_____

Mental Filter: Only paying attention to certain types of evidence and not seeing successes, only failures. Example: "Sure, I paid off my credit card debt, but that doesn't mean I can pay off a mountain of student loan debt."

My mental filter:

_____

_____

_____

Jumping to Conclusions: Imagining you know what others are thinking; predicting the future. Examples: "Getting a part-time job outside my industry means I'm giving up on my career goals" or "If my neighbors find out my parents helped me with a down payment on my car, they'll think I'm a moocher."

My jumping to conclusions:

_____

_____

_____

Overgeneralizing: Seeing a pattern based on a single instance or being overly broad in drawing conclusions. Examples: "Last time I gambled, I played at this table and won, so I'm going to only play at this table" or "Every time I try to do an elevator pitch, I mess up, so it's not worth trying anymore."

My overgeneralizing:

_____

_____

_____

Emotional Reasoning: Assuming that because you feel a certain way, what you are thinking must be true. Examples: "I don't understand all the credit score factors, so I must be stupid" or "Buying this professional outfit will make me feel more confident."

My emotional reasoning:

_____

_____

_____

Labeling: Assigning labels to yourself or others. Examples: "I'm a fraud for having inherited money" or "I'm a lost cause; I'll never figure out my money stuff."

My labeling:

_____

_____

_____

Personalization and Blame: Taking the blame for something that wasn't entirely your fault or the opposite, excluding yourself and blaming others for something that you did. Examples: "I deserved to lose money in the stock market this year; what was I thinking investing?" or "I was rejected from my mortgage application because I didn't finish college."

My personalization and blame:

_____

_____

_____

Critical Words: Using words like "should" or "must" that can make you feel guilty or like you've already failed. When applying it to others, it often looks like frustration. Examples: "I shouldn't have taken out as many student loans" or "She must have known that inviting me to go shopping would mean I'd blow my spending plan."

My critical words:

_____

_____

_____

Magnification and Minimization: Blowing things out of proportion or decreasing the importance of something. Examples: "If I stop spending money on entrepreneur webinars, I'll lose the opportunity to get any new clients" or "Seeing a financial planner is a waste of time."

My magnification and minimization:

_____

_____

_____

Disqualifying the Positive: Discounting the good things that have happened or believing they don't count. Example: "I only got the raise because the company was under scrutiny for employee management."

My disqualifying the positive:

_____

_____

_____

DECISION FATIGUE

Have you ever gone to a restaurant where they handed you a menu and it was more like a small book? You scanned page after page of starters, salads, wraps, entrees, and side dishes, and found your eyes starting to blur. Every time the server came over asking "Are you ready to order?" you felt yourself start to panic. You thought, "Ready? I'm only on the second page and I have twelve more to read!"

Compare that experience with a restaurant that hands you a one-sided menu with two appetizer options and three entree options. When the server asks if you're ready to order, you can confidently order what you want.

We think we want lots of choices. However, we are already making TONS of decisions every single day (35,000 decisions on average by the time our heads hit the pillow). Because we have so many things thrown at us, our brain quickly gets exhausted and we start making rash decisions just to be done thinking about weighing choices. The more choices you have to make, the harder it is for your brain to make these choices. Decision fatigue is what happens when you are low on mental energy after making choices throughout the day. In other words, the more choices you have to make, the worse you'll be at making an informed, educated decision.

Roy Baumeister, a famous researcher in the field of decision fatigue, said that structuring our lives helps us to create routines so we can conserve our mental energy. Barack Obama famously ate nearly the same thing every day when he was sitting president. Anna Wintour has worn the same hairstyle since she was fourteen years old. Mark Zuckerberg essentially wears a uniform of jeans and a gray T-shirt. They do these things to cut down on the amount of choices they have to make throughout the day. Baumeister suggests creating downtime in between meetings, avoiding all-you-can-eat buffets, and setting up regular workout appointments to help conserve your decision-making power.

Let's apply this knowledge to financial decision-making. When it comes to keeping our financial anxious thoughts at bay, eliminating unnecessary decision-making with the following techniques can be helpful.

- Delegating tasks. Delegating tasks is offloading repetitive tasks or things that you aren't great at. With technology, it's easier than ever to delegate. With a few taps on your mobile banking app, you can automate saving. You can set rules like "round up to the nearest dollar" anytime you swipe your debit card to instantly start putting change toward a savings goal.

- Creating rules or boundaries. This is a great way to make fewer decisions (think of Obama and his food).

- Creating daily routines. This means your brain has less to think about because certain tasks have become habits. Just like you brush your teeth without thinking, you can create a routine that includes a financial task.

Making big choices earlier in the day. Earlier in the day, your brain hasn't been "on" all day. Studies have found that prisoners asking for parole are more likely to be granted parole by a judge in the morning than in the afternoon.[4]

Let me illustrate with an example of a person who could benefit from delegation to reduce her decision fatigue.

> Amile is a classic Doomsday Prepper. To feel like she is organized enough with her finances, she spends each Sunday in an elaborate routine with her finances. She writes out all of her spending and cross-checks it against the transactions on her debit card. She highlights every expense with one of three colors: yellow for "okay amount to spend," blue for "you need to cut back," and orange for "yay, you underspent!" From there, she transfers all of the blue-highlighted expenses onto a spreadsheet. If something like "internet" ends up there, she searches for new packages or providers that can lower her cost.
>
> It's not uncommon for this "quick" twenty-minute Sunday ritual to turn into a several-hour rabbit-hole of researching for ways she can save a dollar or two. The problem is that even after she saves by switching to a new internet service provider, she doesn't have any sort of baseline she's using to determine which expenses are okay and which are too much. She checks in against what she thinks is an okay amount to spend. This means that week after week, all of her highlighted blue categories that are "fixed" one week can easily end right back on her blue list, creating an exhausting cycle of constant searching for ways to scrimp and save. Because she spends every Sunday evening using her brain's limited capacity to make financial decisions, she often ends up exhausted and overwhelmed. This feels terrible to her because as a Doomsday Prepper, she really hopes that at the end of her Sunday ritual she'd come away feeling confident and prepared, but she usually ends up feeling the opposite.
>
> Contrast this Sunday ritual with Amile's new ritual after implementing tools to help her reduce her financial decision fatigue. She started by linking her debit card to a spending app. She set weekly spending limits on the app for each category. Now, all she has to do on Sundays is look at her spending. It usually takes her less than five minutes to see where she was able to spend within or below her limit. For the areas she's "overspent," she can now see whether or not the overspending is chronic, or whether she

---

4   S. Danziger, J. Levav, and L. Avnaim-Pesso. "Extraneous Factors in Judicial Decisions," *Proceedings of the National Academy of Sciences* 108 no. 17 (2011): 6889–92.

just needs to cut back for a week or two. This allows Amile to see where her money goes, spend in line with her goals, and make small money tweaks as needed. She feels much better with the automated ritual. With so many decisions lifted off her plate, she is free to spend her energy and decision-making power on more important things.

• REDUCE FINANCIAL DECISION FATIGUE •

Using the techniques on page 29 to help with decision fatigue, review how you can apply those tips to your financial life.

TIP	EXAMPLE	WHAT CAN I DO?
Delegate tasks	Automate bill payments	
Create rules or boundaries	Order takeout lunch once a week	
Create daily routine	Check my spending every Sunday morning	
Make big choices early	When a big purchase is coming up, spend Saturday morning doing research for the best deal. Bonus, set a timer for a specific time I've allotted to researching so I don't get overwhelmed and start second-guessing myself	

ANXIETY AND EMOTIONAL ACTIONS

We've covered how anxiety shows up in our bodies and in our minds. Now, let's talk about the emotional side of anxiety. When anxiety shows up emotionally, it doesn't just look like being worried. While worry is certainly one way anxiety shows up, it can also look like increased irritability, agitation, feeling overwhelmed, increased sense of loneliness or isolation, and an inability to relax. These emotions are often tied to some action or behavior.

Take the case of Nate. Nate swore up and down that he didn't have financial anxiety. However, his husband noticed that twice a month when they were paying bills, Nate had a habit of deep cleaning the kitchen. It was like he couldn't sit still! They'd sit down to review what was due, and Nate would hop up and say things like, "I'll be able to focus once I unload the dish-washer" or "Let me just finish scrubbing the oven." What seemed like a quirk quickly became a routine pattern anytime bills were brought up.

• IDENTIFYING ANXIOUS ACTIONS •

In the space below, write down the anxious actions you find yourself doing when your stress or anxiety is heightened. Various prompts are provided, but feel free to add your own if these don't resonate with you.

Anxious distraction techniques: *Refreshing my phone*

_____

_____

_____

Anxious irritability: *Getting irrationally annoyed when my coworkers are five minutes late, snapping at my kids*

_____

_____

_____

Anxious loneliness or isolation: *Feeling like I'm on an island even when I'm surrounded by people at a party, wanting to stay at work late when everyone is gone rather than go home*

_____

_____

_____

Anxious inability to relax: *Having an urge to get up and move my body, which usually looks like cleaning my car or kitchen*

_____

_____

_____

My additional anxious emotions and actions: *Obsessively double-checking that I paid my bills*

_____

_____

_____

USING CBT FOR ANXIOUS FINANCIAL THOUGHTS, FEELINGS, AND ACTIONS

Dr. Aaron Beck had a student who went on to flesh out his findings. Dr. David Burns deepened the psychology world's view of cognitive distortions and therapy. Now known as cognitive behavioral therapy (or CBT), it is based on the idea that our thoughts, feelings, and behaviors are all intertwined. CBT aims to help a person target one or all of those areas with the goal of stopping and redirecting their anxiety trajectory. We started this chapter identifying how anxiety looks and feels for you. Now, you can take the next step to address it and start to make a change.

The purpose of CBT is to help a person gradually work their way through anxiety-provoking situations. It's often explained with a pool metaphor. Let's say on a hot day you decide to go swimming at the neighborhood pool. Imagine the pool is the thing you're anxious about. When you dip your toe in, the water feels freezing, so you remove your toe and try again later. Wouldn't you know, when you dip your toe in twenty minutes later, it's still cold. The cycle continues: dip toe, water is cold, remove toe, and wait. This is the way many of us approach an anxiety-provoking situation. We approach it, see that it's scary or might be uncomfortable, so we don't go toward it. Let's say you've really committed to getting into the pool. You have a couple of options: you can dive in or you can immerse yourself slowly. With anxiety, if you dive in, what tends to happen is you feel freezing. The water takes your breath away, you quickly hop out of the pool, and you tell yourself, "See, I knew it'd be cold, and it was!" and don't get back in the pool.

The other way into the pool is to take it step by step. You head to the stairs at the edge of the pool and put both feet on the highest step. The water is cold, no doubt, but you stand there for a few moments until the water is no longer so shocking, and you take the next step in. The water is around your shins or knees. Your shins or knees feel temporarily cold, but your feet have already acclimated so you have proof that getting in the water, while uncomfortable, is doable. This happens slowly, and step by step. This, my friend, is how you deal with anxiety. You take it one step at a time, knowing that it'll be a little uncomfortable, but the longer you stay in that discomfort, the easier it becomes until you are fully acclimated.

CBT TRIANGLE

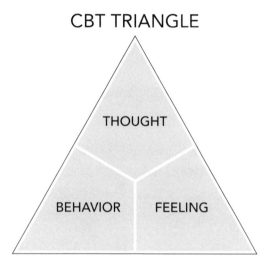

Without CBT Example: Miranda, a classic type A, realized when she got to her friend's house for a book club meeting that she was thirty minutes late. She'd entered the time incorrectly in her phone. "If I walk in late now, everyone is going to think I'm an idiot who can't track time. They'll probably stop inviting me to book club [thought]." Her palms began to sweat, and she could feel the blood drain from her face [feeling]. Rather than face the humiliation of being late, she quietly backed her car out of the driveway and sent a text to her friend that she couldn't make it because she wasn't feeling well [behavior].

Applying CBT Example: Miranda, a classic type A, realized when she got to her friend's house for a book club meeting that she was thirty minutes late. She'd put the time in incorrectly in her phone. "If I walk in late now, they are totally going to tease me! But I've been on time or early for the past eight book clubs [thought]." While she feels her heart racing, she turns off her car, opens the car door to place both feet on the ground, and takes a few deep breaths until she can feel her heart rate start to return to its normal pace [feeling]. She walks into her friend's house, makes a joke about being late, and settles in on the couch next to a friend [behavior].

• REFRAME ANXIOUS THOUGHTS •

This next exercise pulls from CBT and will help you identify your negative thought, examine it with curiosity, and reframe it so you can look at it rationally. We are going to use what we know about cognitive distortions to reframe them from negative or distorted thoughts into neutral or realistic thoughts. Once we identify the cognitive distortion, we are going to look at it with curiosity and objectivity to see how much weight or truth is really in that distorted thought.

DISTORTED THOUGHT: *I don't understand credit scores so I must be stupid (emotional reasoning, labeling).*

> **Proof for the distorted thought:** *I've tried figuring out how to raise my score but get too overwhelmed and stop.*

> **Evidence against the distorted thought:** *I'm not stupid; I finished college and have looked into credit score factors several times.*

> **Realistic thought:** *Even though I get overwhelmed when determining different credit score factors, I know with patience, I'll be able to understand it and work on raising my score.*

DISTORTED THOUGHT: *I can't talk with my spouse about money or they'll think I'm nagging them.*

> **Proof for the distorted thought:** *When I've brought it up in the past, my spouse sometimes gets defensive.*

> **Evidence against the distorted thought:** *My spouse and I have worked through other disagreements. We have the ability to talk and problem-solve without blaming each other.*

> **Realistic thought:** *It's probably best if I bring up money when we are both calm, and start by letting them know we are a team financially.*

DISTORTED THOUGHT:

_____

Proof for the distorted thought:

_____

Evidence against the distorted thought:

_____

Realistic thought:

_____

DISTORTED THOUGHT:

_____

Proof for the distorted thought:

_____

Evidence against the distorted thought:

_____

Realistic thought:

_____

DISTORTED THOUGHT:

_____

Proof for the distorted thought:

_____

Evidence against the distorted thought:

_____

Realistic thought:

_____

LEARN TO CALM YOUR BODY

When your body starts to feel anxious, it sends signals to your mind that we you anxious and are therefore in danger. Your brains then respond to that threat, and your anxiety symptoms increase in intensity. Rather than succumbing to the uncomfortable feeling of an anxiety spiral, check in objectively with your anxious body and try to soothe them or quiet them. While different techniques work for different people, an easy way to practice this in real life is by simply trying to apply the opposite of the anxious feeling you are experiencing. The exercise below helps you do just that.

• USING OPPOSITES TO TACKLE ANXIETY •

As mentioned above, the simplest way to cope with physical anxiety when you are overwhelmed is to ask your body to make the opposite move. Does your jaw feel tense and tight? What's the opposite of that? Loose and relaxed? Great, try reminding yourself to unclench your jaw and relax your facial muscles. Do you suddenly feel the onset of a heat wave before presenting? Grab a cold water bottle to hold onto or take a sip from before presenting. Complete the chart below to collect anxiety remedies.

PHYSICAL SYMPTOM OF ANXIETY	OPPOSITE REMEDY
Tense jaw	Wiggle jaw, invite muscles to relax
Face flushes with heat	Hold onto something cool

•USING LABELING AND LOGIC•

In this worksheet, you will identify the feeling, look at it with curiosity, then offer a different solution to your body. One of the best things you can do when you are feeling an anxious symptom is to simply call it out. Identifying it and giving it a name helps to take away the discomfort because you are able to tap into your logical mind to counteract the anxious symptom. Depending on your comfort level, it can be helpful to call to mind a scenario in which you were feeling physically anxious to illuminate this exercise.

IDENTIFY IT: *My heart is pounding*

Acknowledge it with curiosity: *My anxiety is causing my heart to race. It's probably racing because I'm nervous about my performance review.*

Offer an alternative: *If I take three deep breaths, I can calm my heart and remind myself that I had a great year at work.*

IDENTIFY IT:

_____

Acknowledge it with curiosity:

_____

Offer an alternative:

_____

IDENTIFY IT:

_____

Acknowledge it with curiosity:

_____

Offer an alternative:

_____

IDENTIFY IT:

_____

Acknowledge it with curiosity:

_____

Offer an alternative:

_____

LEARN NEW BEHAVIORS

Remember Nate from earlier? He was the one who couldn't sit still when it was time to pay the bills. While cleaning isn't exactly a harmful way to react to stress, many of us turn toward coping skills that are a temporary fix but don't serve us in the long run. Think of pouring a glass of wine. One drink is probably fine, assuming you aren't in recovery. But if your go-to action when you look at your bank statements is pouring a glass of wine, you are conditioning yourself to associate that glass of wine with money. What does that do to you in the long run? Does it mean you need to drink more when you talk about money? Does it make it uncomfortable to face money issues without a drink in hand? In this exercise, you'll identify what types of things you might be doing when you are experiencing financial anxiety, and brainstorm alternate, positive, and sustainable behaviors.

• PRACTICE LEARNING NEW BEHAVIORS •

ANXIOUS BEHAVIOR: _Feeling on edge or fidgety when it comes time to pay bills, which often looks like me cleaning something in order to avoid looking at bills._

Alternate behavior choices: _Practice grounding, clean one thing before addressing bills, move bills to autopay, only pay bills after having cooked and cleaned a yummy meal._

Winning behavior choice: _Clean one thing before addressing bills._

ANXIOUS BEHAVIOR:

_____

Alternate behavior choices:

_____

Winning behavior choice:

_____

In this chapter, you learned that anxiety is a normal human emotion. While uncomfortable at times, it won't kill you. You have the capacity to learn how to tolerate being uncomfortable, and you are starting to learn ways to reframe your thoughts to quiet the anxious noise in your head.

My top three takeaways from this chapter:

1. _____

2. _____

3. _____

PERSONAL FINANCE 101

"If you are not staying on top of your money, you are putting your financial well-being at risk."

—Suze Orman, financial advisor, author, and television host

I failed my college math class. This class wasn't calculus or math theory. It was entry-level algebra. I'm not exactly the kind of person who thinks math is fun or enjoyable. And yet, I love talking and learning about money. Why? Because money has less to do with math and more to do with mindset, beliefs, feelings, and behaviors.

Money isn't hard. You aren't bad at money because you aren't good at math. And even if you get math, it doesn't mean you should be good at money (interestingly, MANY of my financial therapy clients work in finance, accounting, or lending).

The jargon surrounding personal finance tends to make us feel unintelligent and deceives us into thinking it's hard. In this chapter, I'm going to do a similar version of psychoeducation as I did with anxiety in Chapter 2. The goal of this chapter is to teach you the basic building blocks of money. I want you to understand key terms so you can identify your pain points and feel confident when you interact with your money.

DEFINITIONS

To get comfortable with money, you have to know the basics. In addition to defining some of the basics, I'll include examples to help illuminate the descriptions so that you can ace the fill-in-the-blank quizzes throughout this chapter.

Income and Expenses

Income: This is the money you earn or bring in each month. It includes paychecks, benefits, dividends, government assistance, and court-ordered payouts such as child support or alimony.

Expenses: Anything you have to pay for. Regular monthly expenses would be rent, a car loan, the internet bill, and the phone bill. Things that may fluctuate are eating out, transportation costs, and clothing costs. It's money that is subtracted from your income.

Checking account: A bank account that is designed for frequent transactions. Usually earns low to no interest as money is likely coming in and going out regularly. A good checking account does not have a monthly fee. Make sure yours isn't limiting the amount of transactions you're able to make, or charging you when your balance dips below a certain point.

Savings account: A bank account that earns a small rate of interest on any deposits kept in the account. This account is usually used for short-term savings, so you have money separate from your primary checking or bank account that's still easily accessible.

Emergency fund: Money in a savings account that is easily accessible, to be used only in the case of an emergency. Different financial experts recommend different amounts, but you want anywhere from three to eight months of expenses saved. If you aren't there, start by saving $1,000.

A Note on Emergency Funds

An emergency fund isn't sexy; it's cash that sits in a plain-old, high-yield savings account you can easily access if needed. This money is often used for a deductible if you get in a car accident, unexpected medical expenses, or a flight to visit an ailing relative. Everyone's definition of what constitutes an emergency will be different, though generally, anything you pay for on a semi-regular basis falls outside of this category. A killer sale at your favorite store, lunch out with friends who are in town visiting, and tickets to a Broadway show are NOT emergencies. The baseline for what a person needs in their emergency fund is based on a month of necessary living expenses. As in "my emergency fund will cover me for one month if something happened to me."

Debit card: A card that is linked directly to your checking account. When used, funds are immediately withdrawn from your checking account.

Credit card: A card that is tied to a dollar amount being loaned by a banking institution. The credit card holder agrees to pay that institution back within a certain amount of time, or they will be charged interest.

Cost of living: Amount of money needed in a specific area to be able to pay for basics such as food, shelter, and transportation.

• VOCABULARY QUIZ •

Fill in the blanks using your newly sharpened financial vocab: expenses, checking account, income, savings account, debit card, credit card, emergency fund, savings account, cost of living

Amount of money needed in a specific geographic area to be able to pay for basics _____

A card that is linked directly to your checking account, from which funds are immediately withdrawn _____

An account that is designed for frequent transactions _____

Money in a savings account that is easily accessible to be used only in the case of an emergency _____

Anything you have to pay for _____

A card that is tied to a dollar amount being loaned by a banking institution _____

Any money you earn or bring in each month _____

An account that earns a small rate of interest on any deposits kept in the account _____

GET TO KNOW YOUR DOLLARS

This is a great time to take a look at your numbers, practice the grounding exercises from Chapter 1, and practice some of the cognitive reframing exercises from Chapter 2. I almost always start my financial therapy sessions by having clients look at their income and expenses by filling out a log like the one below. It's simple—not easy—to know what is coming in and going out. Let me explain. Have you heard of the health benefits of regular, quality sleep? Sure you have, it's simple, just get seven-and-a-half to eight hours of sleep every night. But is it easy to do? No, because life gets in the way. You have every intention of going to bed at 10:30 p.m. and waking up at 6 a.m. You get home from work around 7:30 but you want to get a workout in. After getting to the gym and back, it's now closer to 9 p.m. You have to take the dog on a walk, and now it's 9:30 p.m. Still no dinner, you rush down the street to get some healthy-ish takeout, and finish eating by 10:15 p.m. You quickly pack leftovers for lunch and look at the clock—10:30 p.m. You haven't even connected with your partner about your day, and you both want to wind down with a quick show on Netflix. Now? It's 11:30 and your mind and body are still racing from the day you've had. So, is it "easy" to go to bed at 10:30 as planned? No, but in theory, it's simple.

Getting back to simple vs. easy when managing your money, it's simple to know you should spend less than you earn. The first step is to know your numbers if you want to take control of your financial anxiety. Knowing your monthly income and expenses are the building block on which most personal finance begins. To get started, you have a few options. If you are already tracking your spending with an app or paper and pen, you are in good shape. If not, track everything you earn and spend for one week and then come back to this exercise.

• SPENDING LOG AND QUESTIONS •

Track every single thing you spend money on for one week If you are using a spending app, transfer a week's worth of numbers to this log. After tracking your spending for a week, answer the corresponding questions.

DATE	ITEM	EXPENSE

Were any expenses higher than you'd anticipated?

_____

_____

_____

_____

_____

Were any expenses lower than you'd anticipated?

_____

_____

_____

_____

_____

What surprised you about tracking your spending?

_____

_____

_____

_____

_____

What feelings came up as you tracked your spending?

_____

_____

_____

_____

_____

• SPENDING PLAN •

A spending plan, also called a budget or cash flow, is a way to know what money you have coming in and what money is going out monthly. In this worksheet, you'll subtract the amount of money you spend each month (expenses) from your income to get an idea of how much more or less you are spending than you earn each month. Is your head spinning yet? I hope not. This is honestly where I see clients get the most frustrated when starting out. However, I also find they seem to be the most relieved or thankful after finishing and continuing their spending plan worksheets. Pause and take deep breaths as frequently as needed.

Remember, you could be getting money from your nine-to-five, your side hustle, child support, etc. Anything you bring in is income. Expenses, as discussed above, are anything you spend money on. The great thing about a monthly spending plan is that you can spend on more than just the necessities needed to survive. This is where things like the *NY Times* subscription, lattes, new clothes, and the like come into play. Saving for retirement, an anniversary trip, or a new couch would also be counted in your spending plan.

INCOME SOURCE #1		ROTH RETIREMENT CONTRIBUTION	
INCOME SOURCE #2		SAVINGS, EMERGENCY	
INCOME SOURCE #3		SAVINGS, GOALS	
BOX 1 TOTAL:		BOX 2 TOTAL:	

Expenses

Housing (rent/mortgage)	
Transportation (car payment or public transportation)	
Gas (if you own/lease a car)	
Groceries	
Household gas	
Water	
Electricity	
Car insurance	
Homeowner's/renter's insurance	
Health insurance	
Toiletries	
Travel	
Clothes	
Donations/charity	
Dining out	
Pet care	
Cell	
Cable/internet	
Streaming service	
Childcare/daycare	
Tuition	
Student loan	
Gifts	
Grooming	
Other:	
Other:	
Other:	
BOX 3 TOTAL:	

BOX 1	
+ BOX 2	
SUBTOTAL	
- BOX 3	
BOX 4 TOTAL:	

What are you to do with this info?

If you have a positive number in box 4, good for you! You are living below your means or spending less than you earn. You want to stay here so you can have a cushion. Living below your means gives you breathing room for the realities that life sends your way.

If you ended up with a zero or close to zero, don't freak out. There are ways to get your spending to be less than your income. We will get there as this book continues, as I'm a firm believer that spending and saving in line with your values will go farther and be more consistent than randomly slashing a Netflix subscription and foregoing the occasional brunch, as many personal finance experts recommend. I'm a huge proponent of increasing your income in tandem with decreasing your expenses. You can only cut so much from a budget, but you can always, and yes I mean always, earn more.

NOW-WE-ARE-GETTING-FANCY TERMS

You did it! You've got the basics of personal finance down! Ready to learn more? This next round of terms will help you when it comes to getting a loan, choosing a credit card, and figuring out what is best for you and your financial goals. Knowing what these terms are and how to apply them can help you feel more in control as you navigate financial ventures. You won't have to pretend to nod along when you are signing on a new (or new-for-you) car when they get to various line items. You'll know what they mean and have the confidence to ask smart, empowering questions.

Interest: A fee paid when you are borrowing money, whether in the form of a loan or credit. You pay it when you borrow money; you earn it when you invest money.

Interest rate (sometimes referred to as annual percentage rate, or APR): The agreed-upon cost of borrowing money or the return rate of having invested or saved money. There are fixed interest rates, which stay the same throughout the life of the loan, and variable interest rates, which change along with the economy.

Compound interest: This is where interest earned over a certain period is rolled in with the principal before the next interest payout is calculated; it's commonly applied to savings and investments. For instance, if you deposit money and it earns a certain amount of interest, that amount is added onto the deposit amount for the next interest assessment.

> Julia Lynn puts $1,000 in a savings account that is paying her 1% interest. The interest is compounded once a year. After a year, Julia Lynn has earned 1% on her $1,000, bringing her new balance to $1,010. If she leaves that amount in the account and continues to earn 1% interest, she'll earn 1% on $1,010 during the next year for a new total of $1,020.10.

> Julia Lynn wants to earn more than 1% interest and invests in an index fund. That index fund averages a return of 8%. She invests $1,000 and at the end of the year has a total of $1,080. Better than that $1,010, right? To really demonstrate the power of compound interest, let's look at what happens if she contributes $300 a month to that original $1,000 for thirty years, earning that 8% interest rate. In thirty years, she'd have $450,507.78, compounding annually.

The takeaway? Compound interest can be your best friend if you are earning it or your worst nightmare if you are paying it in the form of loan repayment or credit card debt.

Asset: Any item that has significant cash value to the extent it could be sold. This often includes property, vehicles, fine art, certain collectibles, investments, and jewelry. It doesn't include things like clothing or everyday household items.

Bear market: An economic market condition where stock prices are dropping and key economic indicators are poor.

Bonds: This is a type of investment where you effectively loan money to a government or other entity at a fixed interest rate for a certain period of time. After that period, the money loaned plus the interest earned is repaid. Bonds can be issued by private companies, states, the federal government, or foreign governments.

Bull market: An economic market condition where stock prices are rising, investment opportunities are strong, and key economic indicators are good.

Depreciation: Decreasing the value of an asset over a given time. This means you can't sell the asset for as much as you purchased it for initially.

Dividends: The money a company pays to its shareholders when the company earns a profit. When the company does not profit, dividends may be paid out of a company's reserves.

Index fund: Essentially the same thing as a mutual fund, except that it is passively managed, usually meaning it has a lower fee associated with it. This mirrors the stock market index.

Investment: This is anything purchased to earn a profit or get a payout. This can be a financial entity, such as a stock or bond, or a physical entity such as a piece of property or a particular item that you anticipate will gain value over time.

Liabilities: This is a fancy name for debts owed. It's essentially the money that you owe to lenders and creditors, including any remaining balances owed on loans related to asset purchases.

Lien: A legal designation that retains ownership of an asset until a debt is discharged. Basically, if a lien is placed against an asset, you cannot legally sell or get rid of that asset until your debt is paid off. The most common lien issue comes with tax liens placed against your home.

Net worth: The amount left after subtracting your liabilities from assets. For example, if Raymundo's paid-off house was valued at $300K and he had student loans and a car loan totaling $200K, his net worth would be $100K (assets minus liabilities).

Money market account: A specialized type of savings account that usually requires a higher deposit and balance, but also offers a higher interest rate. Also known as a money market deposit account (MMDA) or money market savings account.

Mortgage: A loan taken out on a piece of property. It allows consumers to purchase property and pay for it over a period of time, usually anywhere from fifteen to thirty years. There are a variety of different mortgages available depending on your financial situation and credit score.

Mutual fund: This is an investment program funded by shareholders that is actively managed by a third-party service provider. When you invest in a 401(k) or IRA, the money you contribute is usually divided between different mutual funds in order to generate returns on your investment.

Shareholder (often used interchangeably with stockholder): A person who owns at least one share of a company's stock.

• VOCABULARY MATCHING •

Asset	Shareholder	Bull Market	Mortgage
Liabilities	Dividend	Bear Market	Mutual Fund
Net Worth	Investment	Lien	Index Fund
Depreciation	Bonds	Money Market Account	

_____ An economic market condition where stock prices are dropping and key economic indicators are poor

_____ Any item that has significant cash value to the extent it could be sold

_____ A person who owns at least one share of a company's stock

_____ A type of savings account that usually requires a higher deposit and balance, but also offers a higher interest rate

_____ A loan taken out on a piece of property

_____ This is a type of investment where you loan money to a government or other entity at a fixed interest rate for a certain period of time

_____ An economic market condition where stock prices are rising, investment opportunities are strong, and key economic indicators are good

_____ A legal designation that retains ownership of an asset until a debt is This is an investment program funded by shareholders that is actively managed by a third-party service provider

_____ Passively managed fund that mirrors a specific stock index

_____ This is anything purchased to earn a profit or get a payout

_____ Money owed to lenders and creditors

_____ The money a company pays to its shareholders when the company earns a profit

_____ The amount left after subtracting your liabilities from assets

_____ Decreasing the value of an asset over a given time

_____ Someone/another entity that retains ownership of an asset until a debt is paid.

RETIREMENT

Do not skip this section because you think retirement is far away or you can deal with it later. No matter your age, but especially if you are under 35, you need to start investing in your retirement. Why do you need to save, or as my friend and fellow money author Erin Lowry reminds me, invest for retirement? Simply because you don't want to run out of money in old age. There is almost no such thing as investing too much for retirement. There are many different ways to calculate what you'll need when you are no longer in the workforce. Factors that impact how much you'll need when you clock out for the last time include the cost of living of the location you retire in, your health, your age, how active you plan on being, if you plan on traveling, how much you plan to give to charity, whether or not you own a home or rent, etc. Every financial guru will have a different rule of thumb for retirement, which makes it incredibly confusing and frustrating when trying to figure out how much money you should have saved for retirement. The guidelines listed below are merely that, guidelines.

Multiply your annual salary (pretax)

Age 30: 1x annual salary

Age 35: 2x annual salary

Age 40: 3x annual salary

Age 45: 4x annual salary

Age 50: 6x annual salary

Age 65: 10x annual salary

Though the idea of accumulating ten times your salary might seem overwhelming, if you save and invest early and consistently, you have the benefit of compound interest on your side. The fantastic thing about saving for retirement is that anything, $100 a month, is better than nothing. Refer back to the compound interest example if you need a reminder on the importance of this. Start now if you haven't already.

Retirement Definitions

Retirement: When a person no longer works for an income.

Target date fund: An index fund that automatically rebalances based on the estimated year of a person's retirement. It is riskier, or stock heavy, earlier on and transitions to being more conservative, or bond heavy, closer to the retirement year.

Individual retirement account (IRA): A retirement account funded by you, not an employer.

Thrift savings plan (TSP): A retirement savings account for federally employed workers.

401(k): A for-profit employer-sponsored retirement account where you can invest pretax dollars from your paycheck.

403(b): An employer-sponsored retirement account where you can invest pretax dollars from your paycheck. Nonprofits and schools typically offer these. From a consumer standpoint, there's no difference between a 403(b) and a 401(k).

Roth: A type of investment account where you invest your money after paying taxes. You are not taxed when you access the funds. You can have a Roth IRA or a Roth 401(k). Fun fact: the name comes from Delaware Senator William Roth, who helped to spearhead this in the Taxpayer Relief Act of 1997.

Employer match: When an employer contributes additional money to your qualified retirement plan.

● FILL IN THE BLANKS WRAP-UP ●

Put all of the things you learned in this chapter together for an adorable little story. This exercise is like Mad Libs but for your money! Use any of the financial terms we've covered up to this point to complete the story

Benjie was feeling really good about his money. He'd recently started a new job at a large marketing and advertising agency, and in addition to a higher income, he found out his employer would do an _____ to help him max out his _____. In addition to their contribution, he'd have the option to buy the company's stock at a discounted price, allowing him to be a _____.

He did some quick math and found out that within a few months, he'd meet his goal of having a 3-month _____ in a savings account. Benjie also found a reputable company that could help him refinance his student loans for a lower _____, which would decrease his monthly payment, freeing up some money to pay down his credit card debt, his only remaining _____ outside of his student loan.

KEY

Benjie was feeling really good about his money. He'd recently started a new job at a large marketing and advertising agency and in addition to a higher income, he found out his employer would do an employer match to help him max out his 401(k). In addition to their contribution, he'd have the option to buy the company's stock at a discounted price, allowing him to be a shareholder.

He did some quick math and found out that within a few months, he'd have met his goal of having a 3-month emergency fund in a savings account. Benjie also found a reputable company that could help him refinance his student loans for a lower interest rate, which would decrease his monthly payment, freeing up some money to pay down his credit card debt, his only remaining liability outside of his student loan.

My top three takeaways from this chapter:

1. _____

2. _____

3 _____

CHAPTER 4

VALUES

"Every time you spend money you are casting a vote for the kind of world you want."
—Anna Lappé, sustainable food author and advocate

How are you doing? So far, we've covered your money story, the building blocks of coping with anxiety, and personal finance essentials. If you have tried to learn more about personal finances but find your eyes glaze over—good news! We're about to deep-dive into the emotional side of your money.

In addition to our money stories being formed by our families and communities, our culture plays an enormous role in how we relate to our money. One of the biggest disservices to millennials was being sold some version of "Do what you love, and the money will follow." This Instagram-filtered BS has sold the idea that living a minimalist life, traipsing the country in a refurbished VW van can make you boatloads of money because . . . you followed your "passion" of driving around and nailing your selfie angle (no shade if that's you, you do you). This mentality has set millennials up for a black-and-white way of looking at work and money. One side of the coin says that you have to love your work or you are doing it wrong. The other side means doing a job that you don't like means you aren't living your life the way you should. This leaves many people feeling like they have to chase their passion or risk feeling like a sell-out. I've had countless people sit in front of me say they feel guilty for their pretty decent job because they aren't following their passion for crocheting sweaters for ferrets. Guess what? Sometimes, you have to shovel shit.

I'm not saying that you should be in a toxic work environment or stay in a mind-numbingly tedious job for decades. What I am saying is sometimes shoveling shit is necessary to create enough of a financial safety net to leave said shit-job. The above notion has confused a generation of people into thinking that values are the same things as passion. They aren't. In this chapter, we are going to push aside the narrative that has been sold to get you back in touch with you. What is truly important to you, and how and why that is important for interacting with your money.

THE EMOTIONAL SIDE OF MONEY

Research continues to show us that the more we align our lives with our values, the better we feel. The type of therapy that uses this approach is called Acceptance and Commitment Therapy, or ACT. ACT teaches people to learn ways to live healthier, fuller lives, given that there are lots of things in our lives outside of our control that may cause discomfort or pain. This concept directly applies to our money. Spending, saving, and investing in line with our values helps us to feel more balanced in our financial relationship. By shifting our money in line with our values, it can lift those uncomfortable feelings associated with our money. We are going to take some time now to think about what is truly important for you. What values dictate your next moves? What is essential for you to spend your time on?

● FIND MY VALUES ●

We all have values that shape the way that we navigate the world. This exercise serves as a starting point for you to get an idea of what is or isn't essential for you. It can be hard to boil down your values, so I like to encourage you to think about values in different areas of your life. Sometimes, people find that there is a common theme throughout the various life domains that can serve as a reference point moving forward. The following list of values is a starting point. Scan the list and write down three values that are the most important to you in each domain. I've included some questions to help you identify what values may be important to you.

Acceptance	Assertiveness	Bravery	Cleanliness	Community
Accomplishment	Attentiveness	Calm	Cleverness	Compassion
Accountability	Authenticity	Capability	Comfort	Confidence
Adaptability	Balance	Certainty	Commitment	Connection
Alertness	Belonging	Challenge	Common sense	Consciousness
Ambition	Boldness	Charity	Communication	Consistency

Control	Flexibility	Insightfulness	Performance	Spirituality
Cooperation	Focus	Inspiration	Persistence	Spontaneity
Courage	Foresight	Integrity	Playfulness	Stability
Creativity	Fortitude	Intelligence	Potential	Status
Credibility	Freedom	Intensity	Power	Strength
Culture	Friendship	Intuition	Productivity	Structure
Curiosity	Fun	Joy	Prosperity	Success
Decisiveness	Generosity	Justice	Purpose	Support
Dedication	Goodness	Kindness	Quality	Surprise
Dependability	Grace	Knowledge	Reason	Sustainability
Determination	Gratitude	Leadership	Recognition	Teamwork
Dignity	Greatness	Learning	Reflection	Temperance
Discipline	Growth	Logic	Respect	Thankfulness
Effectiveness	Grit	Love	Responsibility	Thoughtfulness
Efficiency	Happiness	Loyalty	Restraint	Thriftiness
Empathy	Health	Mastery	Risk	Tolerance
Empowerment	Honesty	Maturity	Routine	Toughness
Endurance	Honor	Moderation	Satisfaction	Tradition
Energy	Hope	Motivation	Security	Tranquility
Enjoyment	Humility	Openness	Self-reliance	Transparency
Enthusiasm	Imagination	Optimism	Selflessness	Trustworthiness
Equality	Improvement	Organization	Sensitivity	Understanding
Ethicality	Independence	Originality	Simplicity	Uniqueness
Expansiveness	Individuality	Passion	Sincerity	Unity
Fairness	Innovation	Patience	Smartness	Vitality
Fearlessness	Inquisitive	Peace	Solitude	Wealth

Relationships. What's important to you in terms of the way you interact with friends and family? Do you cherish lots of one-on-one time or energetic family reunions? What makes your heart swell?

Value 1: _____

Value 2: _____

Value 3: _____

Personal Growth. What do you value when it comes to learning more about yourself? Do you prefer to challenge yourself with various books and retreats, or are you happy and content with who you are and finding ways to supplement or reinforce what you know?

Value 1: _____

Value 2: _____

Value 3: _____

Career. What type of work do you crave? An environment with lots of team bonding, or something that mimics freelance work with lots of autonomy? What lights you up about Monday mornings?

Value 1: _____

Value 2: _____

Value 3: _____

Health. What is nonnegotiable when it comes to your physical and mental health? What is your ideal style of exercise? High-intensity classes or leisurely outdoor stroll?

Value 1: _____

Value 2: _____

Value 3: _____

Environment and Community. What is important to you about the neighborhood in which you live? Do you prefer an expansive landscape as your backyard or bustling city life? How important is it for you to know, or not know, your neighbors?

Value 1: _____

Value 2: _____

Value 3: _____

Colleen, a busy graduate student, is on a tight spending plan as she can only work so much during her program. While it's tough for her to make ends meet, she knows it's temporary. She identifies strongly with the values of routine, peace, and predictability. While she knows money is tight, she still goes to the drive-through three days a week on her clinic days, and to the coffee shop for $4 coffee and a donut hole. It's not that she doesn't logically understand that the $12/week could be going elsewhere; for her, it's the routine of driving through before clinic. It's the peace she gets those few moments in the car listening to public radio. It's the predictability of how that donut hole will taste and that the coffee will be hot. This is an example of how values can overrule the "logic" of spending.

Common Values. Were there any values that showed up in more than one domain? As you scan the list of values, is there a prominent theme or tone that comes up? For example, maybe you found that the words "fun, spontaneity, and attentiveness" came up, or a theme of "present" or "mindful" did.

Value 1: _____

Value 2: _____

Value 3: _____

• SPENDING IN LINE WITH MY VALUES •

Remember your expenses categories from the last chapter? Take some time here to reflect on what exactly you are spending money on. Is it in alignment with your values? If not, what's a good alternative? Sometimes, there aren't good alternates, and sitting with that can be a part of the process as outlined above.

EXPENSE	ALIGNED WITH MY VALUES?	ALTERNATE OR REFRAME
Travel example	Yes. Typically do long weekends camping with friends. Aligns with my values of community and responsibility	N/A
Clothing example	No. I have been guilty of lots of fast-fashion runs for seasonal wardrobe updates	No more fast-fashion, opt for higher-quality pieces, preferably from thrift stores or sustainably sourced
Housing example	Sort of. I'd prefer a roommate for friendship and thrift but I'm locked into my lease for eight more months	I'm thankful for housing and am looking forward to finding a new apartment in eight months
Housing		
Transportation		
Groceries		
Gas		
Water		
Electricity		
Car insurance		
Homeowner's/ renter's insurance		

EXPENSE	ALIGNED WITH MY VALUES?	ALTERNATE OR REFRAME
Health insurance		
Toiletries		
Travel		
Clothing		
Donations/charity		
Dining out		
Pet care		
Cable		
Internet/streaming		
Childcare		
Tuition		
Student loans		
Gifts		
Grooming		
Other		

PERSONAL ASSETS

As we reviewed in Chapter 3, assets are anything that holds monetary value. When a lot of my clients start this journey toward stopping their financial anxiety, they have a hard time separating monetary assets from personal assets. This goes doubly for those who are Money Admirers. It's important that as you work on your financial anxiety, you continue to separate your net worth from your personal self-worth. Too often, we forget about the nonmonetary assets within us.

• CONSIDER YOUR PERSONAL ASSETS •

In this exercise, I'll encourage you to think of your nonmonetary assets. These may overlap with your values.

What nonmonetary assets do you bring to your career?

_____

_____

_____

_____

_____

What nonmonetary assets do you bring to relationships?

_____

_____

_____

_____

_____

What nonmonetary assets do you bring to your community and environment?

_____

_____

_____

_____

_____

List all other nonmonetary assets:

_____

_____

_____

_____

_____

BEYOND THE MONEY

As we work through the emotional side of money, it's worth thinking about how money is holding you back. This means you think your goals are limited based on how you are currently managing your finances. If you hear yourself saying things like "I'd love to buy a house like that, but I could never afford it" or "I'll never get out of debt," this exercise will be particularly helpful.

• THINKING BEYOND THE MONEY •

Carve out some quiet time alone, perhaps with a drink in hand from Chapter 1 as you do this exercise. Answer the following questions (adapted from The Financial Life Plan by George Kinder).

If money didn't matter, how would I spend my days?

_____

_____

_____

_____

How would I give back if I had more money?

_____

_____

_____

_____

"All the money I'd ever need." What dollar amount comes to mind?

_____

_____

_____

_____

If I knew failure wasn't an option, what would I do for work?

_____

_____

_____

_____

_____

How happy is my 5-year-old self with my current life?

_____

_____

_____

_____

_____

How happy is my 85-year-old self with my current life?

_____

_____

_____

_____

_____

After answering these questions, reread them and reflect on the following questions:

What surprised you about this exercise?

_____

_____

_____

_____

_____

What did you learn about yourself during this exercise?

_____

_____

_____

_____

_____

Which questions were the most visceral for you? Meaning, which ones "hit you in the gut?" Why do you think that is?

_____

_____

_____

_____

_____

START WITH SPENDING

In this section, I'll break down how you can practice spending in line with your values. If you are spending like crazy on take-out meals but value sustainability, there is a good chance you don't feel great about where that money is going. A way to shift spending money on food while adhering to your beliefs on sustainability would be to meal-prep at home. That way, you have the quick convenience of take-out but aren't accumulating paper and plastic waste, not to mention the environmental cost of driving to and from your favorite take-out joint.

Now, some things that we have to spend money on might not perfectly align with our values, no matter how hard we try. When was the last time you felt really great about paying for your student loans? In cases like this, a gentle reframing of the spending category can help. We use reframing in all areas of therapy. For example, when a person was late to work, rather than thinking, "I'm so pissed I'm late," they can try, "I'm thankful I have a job that is flexible enough to accommodate me when I'm running behind." Rather than thinking of paying student loans as being a part of a broken educational system that burdens those without generational wealth (is my bias showing?), what about thinking about the loans differently? Like, thinking about the knowledge you've learned along the way. Or the friendships that attending college afforded you? How can you reframe so it feels a bit more palatable?

These next two exercises will help you reframe your expense categories and then help you see if there are ways that you are spending that aren't in harmony with your values.

• REFRAME EXPENSE CATEGORIES •

Use this as an opportunity to reframe any category that doesn't resonate with you. For some people, calling a spade a spade works out fine, whereas others may need the reframe in order to truly engage. This exercise is adapted from one Bari Tessler used in *The Art of Money: A Life-Changing Guide to Financial Happiness*. Tessler is a pioneer in the field of financial therapy. Her journey started with sensorimotor therapy, which uses the body's signals to help guide you through both past pain and current decision-making. She advocates for reframing money terms that don't resonate.

CURRENT TERM	REFRAMED TERM
Medical debt from knee surgery	Functional Knee
Mortgage payment	Cozy home
Student loan	
Medical debt	
CC debt	
Mortgage/rent	
Car payment	
Clothes	
Toiletries	
Pet care	
Childcare	

SAVING AND INVESTING

How can you save in line with your values? This one is simpler than you may think. Most banks have a mission statement or list out where or how they invest. If their values line up with yours, perfect! You are all good keeping your savings accounts right where they are. If not, and you value community, you may be better off moving your money to a local credit union. Another option is an online savings account. Find ones with lower fees and higher savings account interest rates.

Investing mindfully and in alignment with our values is a tricky balance to strike. On the one hand, it is essential to put your money where your beliefs are. On the other hand, if you only invest in things that precisely align with you, you may not be looking at a diversified portfolio. Like many financial advisors, I recommend doing the bulk of your investing in something like an index or mutual fund. That will do the diversifying for you. If you'd like to do some other investing outside of that, there are plenty of ways to do so. Below, I've listed out some ways you can invest mindfully.

Community investments: Invest directly in your community. This is the same idea as purchasing goods from a local, small business; you are keeping your dollars in your community, thus helping keep wealth, income, and jobs in your community. You can do this by purchasing local real estate, lending to a nonprofit, or investing directly in a local small business. More firms are popping up that are dedicated to helping you invest in your community. They usually have the words "community capital" or "conscious capital" in their mission statement. If you can't find one, you can reach out to your local business development group or community coalition to see if they can point you in the right direction.

Start-ups: Invest in specific, small companies that align with your values. This has become so much easier with the accessibility of crowdfunding. Sites like Indiegogo and Kickstarter are some of the most well-known if you are interested in learning more about investing in start-ups.

Value-based or socially responsible investments: Invest in more prominent companies that adhere to the same values that resonate with you. This could be companies that value gender equality, use alternative energy, or don't test their products on animals. It could also be not investing in companies that expose workers to questionable work environments. These used to be trickier to find, but now most large brokerage firms have tools that allow you to screen out or screen in companies to your liking. Some companies have already created mutual funds that they deem socially responsible.

BEING INTENTIONAL WITH FINANCES

Reviewing these values helps you connect with what is important to you. Notice I said YOU. This brings us back to the beginning of this chapter. If you value autonomy but are in a job chock-full of bureaucracy, you can work on increasing your emergency fund. Once you have a larger emergency fund, you can start searching for a job that better aligns with your values without sacrificing your fiscal safety. In personal finance, I too often see people putting others, such as their community or kids, in front of themselves. Before you can freely donate to charity or pay for your niece's soccer camp, you must first be rock-solid on being able to afford to support yourself and your values. In starting with you, this means getting comfortable with yourself, knowing that you cannot support others financially until you have your financial house in solid order.

FINANCIAL CHECKLIST: ARE YOU READY TO HELP OTHERS?

Below is a checklist of items you need to have in place before you can move to help others. If you haven't met all of the things on the to-do list in one area, this is high time to STOP giving your money to others. You need to meet ALL items in the personal list before you can comfortably contribute to others or your community. How do you measure up?

❏ 3- to 6-month emergency fund

❏ Contribute 10 to 15% to a retirement account

❏ Pay all bills in full and on time

❏ Don't rely on others for financial stability (e.g., your car isn't subsidized by your parents; this is different from getting an inheritance)

❏ Have health insurance coverage

❏ Spend less than I earn each month

My top three takeaways from this chapter:

1. _____

2. _____

3. _____

CHAPTER 5

SEE IT IN ACTION: SPENDING PLANS

"Generate that wealth for yourself and your family, but pour the overflow of those resources into your community."

—Jadah Sellner

I am adamant about the fact that no one personal finance approach will work for everyone. That's why I'm including examples of various ways you can manage your cash flow, or income and expenses, to see which of them work best for you.

50/30/20 PLAN

Who exactly coined this method is up for debate. While popular credit goes to Elizabeth Warren and her daughter Amelia Warren Tyagi, others have used variations of this method.

This is how the plan works: The numbers stand for percentages of how your after-tax income should be spent, with 50% going toward your necessities, 30% going toward your wants, and 20% going into saving OR debt repayment, depending on your situation. Regardless, the 50/30/20 Plan might be for you if:

- You want a concrete guideline for spending that gives you some wiggle room.

- You need help figuring out how much you should be saving.

- You get tripped up on separating needs and wants and often find yourself asking at the end of the month, "Now where the hell did my paycheck go?"

In order to do this, you first must separate your needs from your wants. Needs, according to many in the personal finance world, are things you have to pay for in order to survive. A want is something that is a bonus or nice to have, but not essential. For example, going to the movies instead of watching TV at home.

CATEGORY	NEED	WANT
Housing	Somewhere safe to live	Housing that has additional amenities such as a pool, private room/bathroom, parking, more space than is necessary, etc.
Clothing	Clothing that is appropriate and reasonable	Name-brand clothing, clothing that is a "fad," clothing above and beyond what is needed to live your life
Transportation	A way to get from Point A to B (public transportation, bike, walk, car, etc.)	Transportation that exceeds the bare-bones way to get to and from places. For example, a vehicle with an 8-cylinder engine instead of a 4-cylinder
Food	Nutritious and accessible food	Take out, restaurants, or higher-end food brands
Health	Health insurance, co-pays, and prescriptions	Complementary health services such as acupuncture, Reiki, or personal training
Utilities, including internet	Reliable electricity, water, and internet	The fastest internet package, running AC in the summer
Phone	Reliable phone	New phone model if you have a working phone

EXAMPLE TIME WITH J'NAY

J'nay takes home $4K per month after taxes and lives in a small city. Using the 50/30/20 rule, she'd have to first separate her needs and wants to ensure she is spending in line with the guidelines.

50 = $2,000   30 = $1,200   20 = $800

Here's how J'nay's expenses are divided between needs and wants.

CATEGORY	AMOUNT	NEED	WANT
Rent	$1,300	X	
Groceries	$520	X	
Gym membership	$140		X
Cell	$90	X	
Cable/internet	$80	X	
Streaming services	$40		X
Co-pays for therapy	$40	X	
Metro card	$39	X	
Gas	$175	X	
Car insurance	$220	X	
Renter's insurance	$8	X	
Clothing	$200		X
Nails 2x/month	$80		X
Toiletries, including skincare	$90	X	
Makeup	$35	X	
Laundry	$20	X	
Entertainment	$125		X
Dining out	$320		X
Total:	$3,522	$2,617 50% is $2,000	$905 30% is $1,200

As you can see, her expenses are over the allotted 50/30 guidelines. Thus, J'nay has to review her expenses and cut corners a bit in order to have the recommended 20% to put toward saving.

Is there anything J'nay can eliminate or downgrade to get her numbers to fit the 50/30/20 rule? As a reminder, she has to shift $617 from her "needs" category to her "wants" category (a pretty good problem to have, if you ask me).

_____

_____

_____

_____

80/20 PLAN

If you (like me) get frustrated with the strictness between needs and wants, you may be better off reframing the 50/30/20 plan to an 80/20 spending plan. Let me explain. The true budget stickler would say that monthly massages are a want and not a need. But for that person who travels three out of four weeks of the month for work, that massage may very well be worth it to stave off the long-term consequences of limbs in odd positions (I'm looking at you, budget airlines and rock-hard hotel beds), and provide a mental and physical respite. Therefore, this person might want a bit more wiggle room as the needs and wants category is a bit blurry. That's where the 80/20 plan comes in.

The 80/20 plan is very similar to the 50/30/20 plan in that it operates in terms of percentages, but it allows you to lump together needs and wants. So you can spend 80% of your after-tax income, whether it's on rent or acupuncture.

The 80/20 Plan might be for you if:

- You are more anxious about adhering to rules and the 50/30/20 plan felt too restrictive and/or like you might fail.

- You live in an area with a high cost of living where it isn't reasonable to have your needs be paid by 50% of your income.

• You need help figuring out how much you should be saving.

We'll reuse J'nay's numbers from the previous example. This time, the 50 and 30 will be combined.

80 (spending): $3,200   20 (saving): $800

CATEGORY	AMOUNT
Rent	$1,300
Groceries	$520
Gym membership	$140
Cell	$90
Cable/internet	$80
Streaming services	$40
Co-pays	$40
Metro card	$39
Gas	$175
Car insurance	$220
Renter's insurance	$8
Clothing	$200
Nails 2x/month	$80
Toiletries, including skincare	$90
Makeup	$35
Laundry	$20
Entertainment	$125
Dining out	$320
Total Spent:	$3,522

While J'nay is still over by a little bit, $322 to be exact, now she doesn't have to rigidly categorize her needs versus wants, she simply has to cut back her non-saving spending by $322 to stay in line with the 80/20 rule, and contribute the monies to the 20% savings.

THE KAKEIBO APPROACH

The kakeibo budgeting approach is more of a daily tracking approach with specific categories for tracking. Rather than adhering to personal finance advice or guidelines, you are in charge of what you want to save and spend, and how you'll do it. The idea is to keep a daily and monthly ledger of your income and expenses and at the end of each month, reflect on how that spending made you feel. The end-of-the-month reflection also asks you to check in on what you saved and to think about setting up saving and spending goals for the following month.

This method might be for you if:

• You value responsibility and writing or tracking by hand

• You practice or value practicing mindfulness

• You are intrigued by personal growth and development

• You are interested in trying out financial anxiety coping skills by looking at your money daily and monthly

The four financial categories in the kakeibo ledger system are outlined below:

Survival: Mandatory expenses that can fluctuate slightly from month to month. This category would include your groceries, rent, and utilities.

Extra: Occasional costs that don't happen regularly, such as attending a wedding or a car repair.

Optional: These are your "wants," things you spend money on that could be cut back if needed.

Culture: Purchases that enrich you and your life, such as hobbies and interests. These can include things like museum entrance fees, concerts, and art classes.

Example:

ITEM	CATEGORY	AMOUNT SPENT
Carry-out salad	Optional	$8
Phone bill	Survival	$80
Gas	Survival	$45
Coworker's going away party	Extra	$20
Gardening gloves	Culture	$14
		Total: $167

At the end of each month, reflect on areas of have, save, spend, and improve. Here's the thing with kakeibo. Like most spending plans, it's hard to neatly categorize each spending item. For example, some people might consider a carry-out salad "optional" because you can bring food from home. However, others might consider the carry-out salad "survival" because it is food. Use whichever category feels best for you.

ITEM	CATEGORY	AMOUNT SPENT

Try this tracking method for a week to get a feel for it. Simply transfer these kakeibo categories into a bullet or lined journal.

WEEK DD/MM/YYYY: _____

ITEM	CATEGORY	AMOUNT SPENT

Have. How much money did you have this month? In other words, how much income did you earn?

_____

Save. How much did you want to save this month? Did you? If yes, what helped you achieve those goals?

_____

_____

_____

_____

_____

Spend. How much did you spend this month?

_____

Improve. How can you improve next month? What lessons did you learn?

_____

_____

_____

_____

THE NO-BUDGET BUDGET

The No-Budget Budget, the anti-budget, and the automatic budget are all similar terms for one approach. Popularized by David Bach and Ramit Sethi, the idea is to pay off all of your bills, and yourself by automatically saving and investing, before spending on other things. Many people approach their savings goals or budget by putting their "leftover money" toward their goals. This often results in lower savings rates, accompanied by a thought that sounds like, "Where did all my money go?" When you fund your goals first, you reap the benefit of seeing that you are able to save and live a life that aligns with your values. This budgeting method takes some work up-front, but once you get it going, it's relatively painless and, dare I say, mindless. I'm also biased because this is the approach I've been using since merging accounts with my partner when we got married.

This may be a good plan for you if:

- On paper, you should be meeting your financial goals but there doesn't seem to be money left over at the end of the month to fund these goals

- You want to deal with your money for the least amount of time possible

- You don't want to feel restricted when you spend your "fun money"

How it works:

First, take a look at your past three to six months of expenses. Yup, this is what I meant when I said there is some work up-front. You will start to get an idea of what you are spending your money on. Once you have this idea, you can start to delegate where you want your money to go, or if there are areas you'd prefer to cut back. You'll set up various accounts within your main bank account to be automatically funded throughout the month.

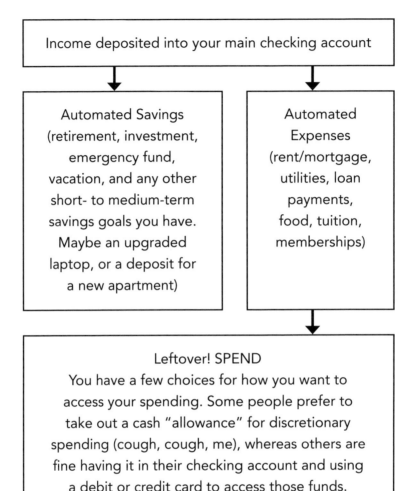

PRO TIP: Set aside time to move all of your bills' due dates to be on the same day of the month. Personally, all my bills are due on the first or the fifteenth of the month. That's easy for me to remember. Even with everything being automated, it can look overwhelming to see so much money moving around on random days throughout the month rather than once or twice. Plus, when money is only flowing out once a month, it's very easy to see if something is wrong. For example, if all of your bills are due on the fifteenth, and suddenly an unexpected amount of money disappears from your bank account on the third, you can quickly spot the potential error.

Research has shown that small language shifts, including financially speaking, help us to feel better about our choices. One small shift that helps people focus on their financial strengths or abundance is simply swapping the word "get" for the word "have" when it comes to spending money. As in, "I get to pay my bills this month" versus "I have to pay my bills this month." By saying that you "get" to spend money on something, you are telling yourself that you have the capability to be able to pay for the things needed to keep your life running. When you say you "have" to spend money on things, it feels more dreaded and negative. I challenge you to try swapping out these words and see what happens!

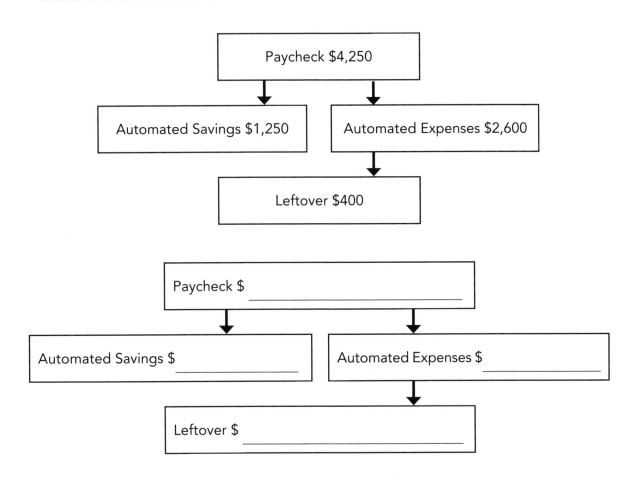

CHAPTER 6

CALMING YOUR BODY AND MIND

"The fact is, inner peace isn't something that comes when you finally paint the whole house a nice shade of cream and start drinking herbal tea. Inner peace is something that is shaped by the wisdom that 'this too shall pass' and is fired in the kiln of self-knowledge."

—Tania Ahsan

What happens when we have anxiety? When we feel those uncomfortable emotions arise and start to notice our thoughts spiraling, we often try to find ways to make that discomfort go away. I've heard and seen various iterations of that discomfort. Some clients physically shudder when they talk about financial anxiety, others verbalize things like, "Ugh, I just HATE that feeling." In this chapter, I'll talk about ways we cope with financial anxiety that aren't necessarily the best and encourage you to find ways to add to your current healthy coping regimen.

First, we'll identify the unhealthy ways that you may be coping with financial anxiety. As you identify your coping skills, especially the ones that I label "unhealthy," it's important to remind yourself that there was a reason you originally adopted that coping skill in the first place. Rather than feeling guilty about employing some less-than-optimal skills, acknowledge that the skill used to help or serve you, and now, you are open to learning new ways to cope. Let's take a look at an example of how a person may have developed unhealthy financial coping skills.

Quinn grew up in a household where money was tight. When anyone in the family had a few extra dollars, they'd shop. Quinn remembers going to the big-box store with his eyes wide open. Everything in the store looked and felt exciting. He remembered holding his parent's hand until they got to the clearance aisle and they'd let him decide what they were going to trade their few dollars for. Sometimes, they'd choose something practical like socks, and other times, they'd go for the novelty pencil eraser or bag of holiday candy. No matter what, Quinn always remembered the feeling of walking up to the cashier and proudly handing over their money to purchase his chosen item. That euphoria and pride would last all day, sometimes through the week.

As an adult in a steady job today, money is no longer tight for Quinn. But on rough days at work or after an argument at home, Quinn continues to hop into his car, credit card ready, to cruise the stores. Rather than only hanging out in the clearance aisle, he now gets the rush of euphoria and pride from outdoor goods stores, organic food stores, and when he's had a really bad day, the electronics store.

As you can see with Quinn, who identifies as a Spender, the impulsive shopping he has as an adult stems from a fond memory of childhood. While swiping his credit card would be seen as an unhealthy way to cope with anxiety or stress, it's easy to see his behavior with empathy when you look at it in context. As you go through the unhealthy coping skills, I encourage you to check in with past experiences that might have led you to employ them.

UNHEALTHY COPING

Unhealthy coping includes anything that may be detrimental to you or others in the short or long term. Common unhealthy ways that people cope with financial anxiety include avoidance, substance use, seeking reassurance, sleeping (too much or too little), isolation, eating (too much or too little), procrastination, ruminating on the problem, compulsive shopping, and gambling. The tricky thing about unhealthy coping is it can be difficult to pinpoint when something goes from an occasional or moderate habit to something that is unhealthy. Shutting yourself away and playing a video games after a rough day at work makes sense. It serves as a distraction and provides a space for you to burn off energy and get lost in a story. Staying up until 2 a.m. playing for the rest of the week, on the other hand, would be unhealthy.

For the purposes of this book, we'll look at the two most common and complained-about coping mechanisms in my financial therapy practice: procrastination and rumination.

Procrastination

As you likely know, procrastination is delaying doing something. This word comes from the Latin words "pro," meaning "forward," and "crastinus," meaning "till the next day." We procrastinate for many reasons. Sometimes we delay things because we are worried we won't be able to do the task or do it right, we think the task won't take too long, or we tell ourselves we'll do it once we complete a more interesting task. We sometimes tell ourselves stories like, "I do better under pressure" or "I get more done when I have more on my plate." Add to those thoughts and ideas the miscalculation of time and you have a recipe for an increase in financial anxiety due to procrastination.

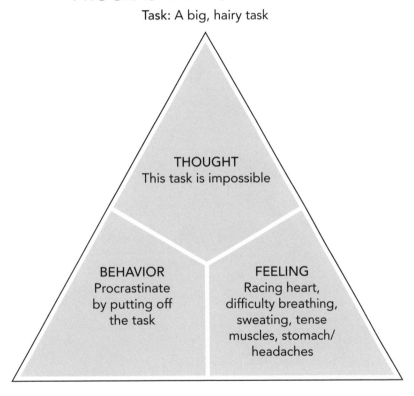

PROCRASTINATION TRIANGLE
Task: A big, hairy task

THOUGHT
This task is impossible

BEHAVIOR
Procrastinate by putting off the task

FEELING
Racing heart, difficulty breathing, sweating, tense muscles, stomach/ headaches

PROCRASTINATION TRIANGLE

Task: Create a spending plan/budget to start tracking spending

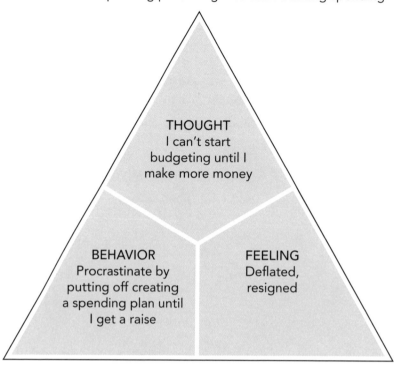

THOUGHT
I can't start
budgeting until I
make more money

BEHAVIOR
Procrastinate by
putting off creating
a spending plan until
I get a raise

FEELING
Deflated,
resigned

Using the example on the previous page, complete the cycle of procrastination patterns you've had when dealing with your personal finances.

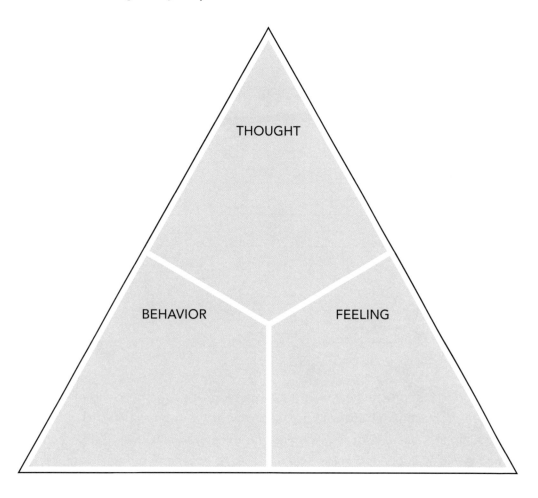

THOUGHT

BEHAVIOR

FEELING

Procrastination vs. Healthy Distraction

Differentiating between healthy distraction and procrastination can be tough. Oftentimes what starts out as healthy distraction slips into procrastination. Ever tell yourself you'll watch "just one episode" on Netflix, only to find yourself sitting in a butt-shaped impression on the couch three hours later? Yeah, that's an example of distraction that turns into procrastination. It's important to know yourself well enough to know how to separate the two.

● IDENTIFY YOUR PROCRASTINATION VS. HEALTHY DISTRACTION ●

As outlined above, we often try to trick ourselves into thinking that we are taking a mental break by distracting ourselves from our anxiety. However, it doesn't take long for that to turn into something unproductive like procrastination. In this exercise, list out exercises or tasks that might be likely to turn into procrastination. Then, set a time limit for healthy distraction so it can stay in the healthy range.

DISTRACTION ACTIVITY	HOW LONG BEFORE IT'S PROCRASTINATION?
Cleaning the garage	Anything over an hour
Watching YouTube	Anything over 25 minutes

Research has found that procrastination is less about time management and more about emotions. We often procrastinate because the temporary, in-the-moment reward of not doing the task (say, scrolling Insta instead of reviewing last month's spending) feels better than facing the task that might make us feel uncomfortable. In order to break the procrastination spiral in the previous exercise, you have to find a reward that feels better than avoidance. This often means turning inward to check with yourself what would feel better than delaying a less-than-fun task.

One of my favorite quick exercises to do with my clients (and personally, if I'm being honest) is asking what your future self would think. Let's say it's a typical Thursday night and you are procrastinating on gathering all of the documents you need in order to get preapproved for a mortgage. You and your partner are going to the credit union first thing on Friday morning. You ask yourself, "What would my 8 a.m. self on Friday think of my actions?" As in, "Do I want to spend some time digging through documentation this evening, or wake up early and scramble to find everything and get out the door on time for the appointment?"

● COACH YOURSELF THROUGH PROCRASTINATION ●

In this exercise, you will identify the reason you are procrastinating and check in with yourself when you feel yourself avoiding an important task.

TASK	WHAT I DO TO AVOID THE TASK	WHAT IT FEELS LIKE TO DO THE TASK
Review last month's spending	Watch Netflix	Overwhelming at first, relief when it's over
Set up appointment with HR to review retirement options	Keep snoozing the HR rep's email	Empowering to start funding my employer-sponsored retirement account

Several things can work when you find your financial anxiety manifesting as procrastination. Research shows simply writing down the task you need to complete can increase your odds of doing said task by 42%.[5] To make this even more impactful, enlist someone who can provide some accountability. See if your partner can remind you to review your spending every Thursday. Ask a friend to attend a retirement seminar through the community college. Having someone else on board or at least reminding you of the task you said you'd wanted to accomplish can help.

---

5   Sarah Gardner and Dave Albee, "Study Focuses on Strategies for Achieving Goals, Resolutions," Dominican University of California News, https://scholar.dominican.edu/cgi/viewcontent.cgi?article=1265&context=news-releases.

• ACCOUNTABILITY PARTNERS •

Who can you identify in your life to hold you accountable? Maybe it's someone at work, a neighbor, or someone you met in an online group. Brainstorm different people who may be able to hold you accountable to decrease the odds that you procrastinate on your personal finance tasks.

DOMAIN	PERSON
Home	Neighbor, partner
Work	Lunch buddy
Home	
Work	
School	
Gym	

Additionally, find ways to start super small. Rather than jumping into something that seems daunting, like "fully fund my Roth IRA by the end of the month," list out the exact steps you have to take to get there. Do each task, one by one, so you can see yourself accomplishing mini-tasks along the way. Breaking things down in this manner helps create a sense of pride and reminds you that you can, in fact, face your financial anxiety and take actionable steps toward quieting it.

• MINI TASKS •

In this exercise, you'll break down what seems like a large, daunting task into bite-size pieces to better set yourself up for success.

Task: Fully fund my Roth IRA

Steps:

- Look up contribution limits for this calendar year

- Calculate monthly contributions needed in order to fully fund Roth IRA

- Ensure my current brokerage account has the option to open a Roth IRA

- Create automatic transfers from my checking account to my Roth IRA account

Task: _____

Steps:

_____

_____

_____

_____

Task: _____

Steps:

_____

_____

_____

_____

Task: _____

Steps:

_____

_____

_____

_____

To take this exercise a step further, are any of the steps that you listed capable of being done in under 15 minutes? If so, ask yourself, can I do this task now? Can I set aside 15 minutes to finish this task? This is like the saying "When it comes to keeping your house tidy, don't put things down, put them away." Review the steps of your tasks above and place a checkmark next to the steps that take 15 minutes or less. Prioritize those the next time you find yourself procrastinating.

Rumination

In cows, rumination is the process of digesting and redigesting food. In humans who don't have multiple stomachs, rumination is more often recognized as thinking and rethinking something, and then, thinking about it some more. We sometimes think doing this is going to help us solve the problem that we are ruminating on. However, much like procrastination, it often only increases our stress or worry without helping us find a productive way to sort out the thing we are ruminating about. Here's an example of how something that on the surface seems like it would help a person get more comfortable with their money turns into a situation full of rumination.

> Jude left the meeting with the financial planner with his head spinning. He is a Blissfully Ignorant money type and had finally made a concerted effort to learn more about the ins and outs of his money. She'd helped him map out a financial plan and gave him a couple of concrete tasks to do before their next meeting. On the walk back to his car, he couldn't stop thinking about the long list she'd mapped out. The words "retirement," "budgeting," "investing," and "life insurance" bounced around in his head to form a congealed worry that became difficult to untangle. By the time he got home, the two

tasks the planner had asked that he do were long buried with the rest of his anxious thoughts.

How to Stop Ruminating

Remember Newton's first law of motion? An object in motion stays in motion. An object at rest stays at rest (this is also why procrastination is so difficult to overcome). Both of these statements are true until you add in an outside force. If your mind is racing and ruminating and thus "in motion," it will continue to stay that way until you find a way to add an outside force to slow down those thoughts until they come to a stop. How can you take a racing thought and slow it down? First, you have to identify it. Then you have to examine it to see what truth is in that thought.

If after identifying and examining the thought, it still isn't going away, it's worth checking in to see if spending time thinking about it is solving anything.

This is a way to interrupt your speeding thoughts by quite literally saying, in your head or aloud, "Stop!" I often say, "Wait!" or "Pause!" My clients know they have to do some work when they hear me say, "Wait, wait, wait, let's pause for a second."

● INTERRUPT RUMINATIVE THOUGHTS ●

Ruminative thought: I'm too far behind financially for any of my planner's advice to make a difference.

Is there anything I can do to change/solve this? YES

If yes, what can I do? Revisit the notes from our meeting. She wrote "Increase retirement contributions by 2%, track spending with an app, and sign up for life insurance" as the top three things I need to do.

Have I done any of these things? NO

Can I do anything about them at this moment? I can't finish them all, but I can download an app to track my spending. On Monday, I'll email HR to learn about increasing my retirement contributions and see if they have information on getting life insurance through work.

Ruminative thought: My financial planner said I need to find cheaper housing, but I'm locked into a lease and I'm walking distance from work. I need to move. I need to find somewhere else to live. But I don't have the cash on hand to break my lease and I don't want to take out a loan or ask someone for money.

Is there anything I can do to change/solve this? NO

How can I release this thought? My lease ends in eight months. In the meantime, I'll focus my efforts on being intentional about my spending, and keep my eyes and ears open for alternate housing in the future.

Ruminative thought: _____

Is there anything I can do to change/solve this? YES

If yes, what can I do? _____

Have I done any of these things? _____

Can I do anything about them at this moment? NO

How can I release this thought?_____

Ruminative thought: _____

Is there anything I can do to change/solve this? YES

If yes, what can I do? _____

Have I done any of these things? _____

Can I do anything about them at this moment? NO

How can I release this thought?_____

Ruminative thought: _____

Is there anything I can do to change/solve this? YES

If yes, what can I do? _____

Have I done any of these things? _____

Can I do anything about them at this moment? NO

How can I release this thought?_____

HEALTHY COPING

Healthy coping skills are those that do not lead to short- or long-term damage for you or others close to you. These skills may look familiar because not only are they helpful for financial anxiety, they are helpful in living a well-balanced life. Some of the more common healthy coping skills fall into these categories: physical, relaxation, emotion-focused, healthy distraction, and time management.

Things like exercise, yoga, cooking, playing with children, and walking would fall into physical coping skills. Reading, massage, aromatherapy, a bath, and drinking tea would be examples of relaxation. Emotion-focused coping skills are journaling, connecting with a partner, practicing mindfulness, or meditating. Healthy distraction might look like watching a favorite sitcom, listening to music, or coloring. Time-management skills include creating firm boundaries for when you allow yourself to work, taking your vacation days, or outsourcing chores.

● DAILY COPING SKILLS ROUTINE ●

To help identify your positive coping skills, reflect on a typical day. Write down the positive, healthy coping skills you may already be doing. Don't worry too much about getting the coping skill in the "right" category. What matters more is that you can see that you are already using healthy coping skills but may have overlooked them

Weekdays

TIME	SKILL
Early morning	Emotion-focused: Deep breathing when I wake up
Morning	Relaxation: Listen to classical music during my commute
Early afternoon	N/A
Afternoon	Relaxation/emotion-focused: Eat a small square of dark chocolate after lunch
Early evening	Physical, healthy distraction: Take the dog for a walk
Evening	Relaxation, time-management: Cook dinner and pack leftovers for lunch
Bedtime	Emotion-focused, healthy distraction: Drink tea and read

What about you? What are things you do that can be added to your list of coping skills?

TIME	SKILL
Early morning	
Morning	
Early afternoon	
Afternoon	
Early evening	
Evening	
Bedtime	

Weekends

Our weekend coping skills might be different from the ones we employ during the week. Complete the daily coping skills routine, this time thinking of what you might do on a typical weekend.

TIME	SKILL
Early morning	Physical: Spinning class
Morning	Physical, emotion-focused: Make breakfast with the kids
Early afternoon	Healthy distraction: Listen to podcasts while doing laundry
Afternoon	N/A
Early evening	Emotion-focused: Neighborhood picnic
Evening	N/A
Bedtime	Emotion-focused, relaxation: Drink tea and read

TIME	SKILL
Early morning	
Morning	
Early afternoon	
Afternoon	
Early evening	
Evening	

TIME	SKILL
Bedtime	

Relaxation

I've had the pleasure of spending time in Europe, where they really know how to relax. On a recent trip to the Netherlands, I found myself feeling quite antsy when going out to eat. It was like the servers were ignoring me! I tried all of the American techniques, making eye contact to cue them that I needed of something, setting my menu down to signal I was ready to order, moving my empty plate toward the edge of the table to say that I was done with my meal and . . . nothing! I watched a few customers around me and they would raise a hand or finger when they needed their server. After a couple of meals, I realized that I wasn't being ignored or getting poor service, I was simply used to the harried pace in which things tend to happen back home. When going out to eat in the States, it isn't uncommon to get your bill while you are still finishing your meal, signaling you to finish your last few bites and move on so someone else can get the table. If you linger after dinner, your server will likely ask you if you need coffee, dessert, or "anything else." But in the Netherlands, like in many parts of Europe, the pace is simply more relaxed. By the end of my visit, I had finally settled into the leisurely pace of dining.

If you are in the States or Canada, you likely have a hard time relaxing. It's not your fault! Our society does a really good job of sending us messaging that if we aren't doing something, we are being lazy. I can name several people who can't watch TV or go to the movies because they feel so restless (and no, this is not because of an ADHD diagnosis). We are conditioned to be on the go, which makes it hard to unwind. It's not uncommon to hear someone say that they feel guilty when they aren't doing something productive. As a healthy coping skill, there are various ways you can practice relaxing.

Deep Breathing

To practice relaxing, you must start with the breath. Most of us are breathing wrong. Yup, wrong. When we are babies, we know how to intuitively breathe, but as we age, we start shifting from deep belly breathing to more shallow chest breathing and spend time "sucking in" our stomachs, which messes with the appropriate way to breathe. According to the American Lung Association, proper breathing starts in the nose and then moves to the stomach as your diaphragm contracts, the belly expands and your lungs fill with air. Breathing this way, "diaphragmatically," is not only the most efficient way to breathe, but it also helps soothe anxiety from a physiological standpoint. Study after study has found that practicing deep breathing, whether in conjunction with a physical practice like yoga or on its own, results in a reduction of sympathetic nervous system activity, or in other words, reduces the negative effects of stress and anxiety.[6]

For this exercise, we will be doing something more physical. Let's relearn how to breathe. The goal is to work your way up to 5 to 10 minutes of deep breathing per day. If you haven't done this before or haven't practiced regularly, note that you may feel a little dizzy when you first start practicing this method of breathing.

1. Lie on your back on a flat surface. You can bend your knees or use a bolster or pillow under them if that is more comfortable. If lying down is uncomfortable or not possible at the time of this exercise, you can sit up straight with your feet on the floor.

2. Place one hand on your upper chest and the other on your stomach, just below your rib cage. Take a few breaths normally and notice how your chest, stomach, and hands rise and fall.

3. Now, breathe in slowly through your nose, inhaling as though you are moving the air toward your lower belly. The hand on your chest should remain still, while the one on your belly should rise.

4. Exhale through your nose or mouth and notice your stomach fall.

5. Repeat 3 to 10 times.

While you will be lying down for this exercise, once you know how to "feel" a deep breath, you'll be able to practice it regardless of where you are or what posture you are in.

Variations on Deep Breathing

Now that you know how to breathe, you can try out these intermediate breathing techniques to help soothe your anxiety.

---

6   X. Ma et al, "The Effect of Diaphragmatic Breathing on Attention, Negative Affect and Stress in Healthy Adults," *Frontiers in Psychology* 8 no. 874 (2017), doi:10.3389/fpsyg.2017.00874.

● BOX BREATHING ●

This exercise is named Box Breathing because it has four "sides."

1. Using the deep breathing technique, inhale for a count of four, hold your breath for a count of four, exhale for a count of four, and hold your breath for a count of four.

2. Repeat this 3 to 10 times.

● MORNING STRETCH ●

1. Upon waking up, sit up with your feet on the floor.

2. Practice a few deep breaths, then add some gentle movement to your breathing. On an inhale, sweep your arms up and overhead. On an exhale, allow your arms to circle back to your sides or to the bed.

3. Repeat 3 to 10 times.

● ALTERNATE NOSTRIL BREATHING ●

1. Close your mouth and breathe in and out of your nose.

2. Close your right nostril with a finger or thumb. Inhale and hold.

3. As you hold your breath momentarily, move your finger or thumb to your left nostril and exhale.

4. Repeat 5 to 10 times.

Physical Relaxation

Wouldn't it be nice to check in with the signals your body is sending in a way that feels good for you? Sensorimotor therapy helps people take notice of their bodies and its signals. Think of the exercises you've already learned, such as grounding. The point of grounding, aside from recalibrating your nervous system, is that the more you practice it, the more you get a feel of what is "normal" for your body.

Sensorimotor therapy is a type of somatic therapy, meaning it is centered on the mind-body connection. It was founded in the 1970s by Pat Ogden and Peter Levine to treat trauma and expand work with clients who had difficulty verbalizing their thoughts and feelings. It can be hard to imagine in today's world that there was a time when medicine didn't include the mind-body connection. According to the Sensorimotor Psychotherapy Institute, Ogden was working as a yoga instructor and dance teacher when she started to notice the connection between movement and mood.

Sensorimotor therapy can be helpful in trauma settings, but now, therapists also use it for depression, anxiety, and attachment concerns. I use it a lot with clients who feel financial anxiety in a more physical way.

As you did in Chapter 1, grounding is one way you can physically relax. To go a bit deeper, I'll borrow from the sensorimotor therapy technique to help you identify the signals your body is sending you to see if there is a what or why behind your physical financial anxiety.

• IDENTIFYING THE BODY'S SIGNALS •

Before you try to identify anxious feelings, it can sometimes be helpful to check in with more neutral or positive feelings. Let's start there.

How do I feel physically right now?

I feel pretty relaxed. My stomach feels neutral, my muscles aren't tense, and my facial muscles are calm.

Why do I think that is?

I had a relatively stress-free day at work and am meeting a friend at the gym in an hour.

How do I feel physically right now?

_____

_____

_____

Why do I think that is?

_____

_____

_____

Now, let's move into some of the more uncomfortable feelings that come along with financial anxiety.

How do I feel physically when I open my bills?

_____

_____

_____

Why do I think that is?

_____

_____

_____

How do I feel physically when I check my credit score?

_____

_____

_____

Why do I think that is?

_____

_____

_____

How do I feel physically when I go out to dinner and pay the bill?

_____

_____

_____

Why do I think that is?

_____

_____

_____

How do I feel physically when I donate change to a collection bucket?

_____

_____

_____

Why do I think that is?

_____

_____

_____

How do I feel physically when I give a gift of cash to a relative or friend who is getting married?

_____

_____

_____

Why do I think that is?

_____

_____

_____

How do I feel physically when my paycheck is deposited into my bank account?

_____

_____

_____

Why do I think that is?

_____

_____

_____

How do I feel physically when I know I have to talk to my parents about their poor financial management?

_____

_____

_____

Why do I think that is?

_____

_____

_____

Feel free to add in your own financial scenarios:

How do I feel physically when

_____

Why do I think that is?

_____

_____

_____

How do I feel physically when

_____

Why do I think that is?

_____

_____

_____

How do I feel physically when

_____

Why do I think that is?

_____

_____

_____

CALMING YOUR MIND

Now that you've had an opportunity to practice calming your body with deep breathing and other relaxation techniques, let's tackle that anxious mind of yours. I've talked about cognitive behavioral therapy before, the idea that our thoughts, feelings, and behaviors are intertwined. In this exercise, you'll be your own therapist. You'll be taking a look at your financially anxious thoughts and seeing how much truth they contain. The goal is to look at your thoughts with an objective lens, the way you might if you were offering advice to a friend.

• FINANCIAL ANXIETY THOUGHT LOG •

SITUATION	DISTORTED THOUGHT	EVIDENCE FOR THE THOUGHT	EVIDENCE AGAINST THE THOUGHT	REFRAMED THOUGHT
Overspent on personal care for the week after staying on track for three weeks	I can't ever stick to a spending plan. I'm such an idiot.	Overspent on personal care	Adhered to my spending plan for three weeks	I was successful 75% of the time and know how to plan for next month

As I've mentioned, writing down your goals can help to hold you accountable. Before we move onto the next chapter, reflect on what you've learned about yourself in this chapter, and think about takeaways and how you can implement these exercises.

What I've learned about myself in the Calming Your Body and Mind chapter.

_____

_____

_____

_____

_____

How can I implement these exercises regularly?

_____

_____

_____

_____

_____

My top three takeaways from this chapter:

1. _____

2. _____

3. _____

CHAPTER 7

BEING SOCIAL WITH FINANCIAL ANXIETY

"Work to maximize the joy we get per dollar spent."

—Ashley Feinstein Gerstley

Having a social life means spending time with friends and family. While it'd be great if the default hangouts were entertaining, fun, and free, the reality is most activities that involve others also involve spending money. As you likely know by now, there is nothing wrong with spending money if you have it and are spending it in a way that feels good for you. But if you are trying to cut down on your spending, whether to practice spending in line with your values or to put additional funds toward debt or saving, it can be hard to verbalize that to others. This chapter is dedicated to helping you maintain your relationships while you alter your spending habits.

When you change your spending habits, particularly if you are spending less than you used to, others will interpret that choice with their money story in mind. If you are spending less, a friend who grew up cutting coupons to get by may scoff at the idea that you'd willingly spend less when you don't "have to." If you have a group of friends whose activities revolve around chasing the newest restaurants in town, don't be alarmed when they suddenly stammer when you invite them over for a potluck.

In this chapter, I'll show you how to have fun without always reaching for your wallet, how to have those awkward social conversations, and how to figure out how to incorporate affordable activities into your life for the long run.

HOW TO HAVE FUN WITHOUT REACHING FOR YOUR WALLET

Do you remember the days in your early twenties when you'd go over to a friend's house just to watch a TV show? You didn't bring a bottle of wine or a charcuterie platter, you brought yourself and maybe a blanket. I'm not advocating for a continued version of your 20-something lifestyle. But something interesting happens as we age and start to make more money. "Lifestyle creep" or "lifestyle inflation" is when a person starts spending more money once they start earning more money. Instead of TV premiere nights, the go-to activities start to become things like happy hours, museum exhibitions, and concerts. It makes sense as that's what society pitches to us as a part of being an adult. But how are you to connect with those you love without spending money? I want to show you how you can socialize without constantly reaching for your wallet, or more realistically, without tapping on Google Pay.

List of Favorite Free Activities

Below are some of my favorite activities. With the beauty of the internet and social media, I sought my friends and Instagram followers to get their favorite free or low-cost things to do and am also sharing them with you below to serve as a starting point, inspiration, and options.

- Donation-only museums

- Going to the lake

- Yoga at home or in the yard

- Watching TV with friends

- Hiking or walking in the park

- Board games

- Catching up over coffee or tea

- Ice cream dates

- Libraries. Most libraries now offer SO much more than books. At my local library, in addition to books, they can get you started with a book club kit, you can rent art for a month, check out movies, get discounts to local attractions, use their computers and printers, join a club, attend free workshops, and more!

- Potlucks

- Going to the local cosmetology school for discounted salon services

- Cookie swap

- BBQs with yard games

- Attending Meetups

- Clothing swap instead of clothing shopping

- Using city Parks & Recreation services. This past summer, I found my city pool offers "dive in" movies, where you can bring a tube, float in the pool, and watch an outdoor film. They also have an annual "doggy day," where on the last day before the pool closes for the season, you can bring your pup for a dip!

- Going to free movies. My city has several theaters that offer free films, usually on Sundays, to the public. Check out local clubs, too, as they often sponsor free screenings of movies that are of interest.

PAID ACTIVITY AND FREE ACTIVITY

In this exercise, I'm going to encourage you to think about common social activities or spending habits you currently engage in and challenge you to think about an alternative that doesn't cost as much. Not only is this a great way to save some money, but it's also a good way to get out of a social rut, so to speak. In Chapter 6, we looked at different coping skills. Socializing can provide a ton of emotional and psychological benefits, so by bulking up the different ways you can socialize, you are also adding to your list of coping skills. Reference the previous list of free activities if you need help. Note, this exercise tends to be relatively easy for Doomsday Preppers and more challenging for Spenders.

CURRENT ACTIVITY	ALTERNATIVE ACTIVITY
Mani/Pedi	*DIY mani/pedi at home and/or with friends*
Going out to eat	*Hosting a dinner by recreating your favorite take-out meal*

CURRENT ACTIVITY	ALTERNATIVE ACTIVITY

GAMIFY IT

How can you WIN at your money when it comes to being social with your friends? A little competition, of course! "Gamifying" something means applying the typical elements of a game—scorekeeping, competition, creating and adhering to rules—to other areas of activity. Research shows that gamifying things can make it more likely that a person will improve their learning (think about being in school and the games teachers would include with lessons) and boost performance. Consider a way that you all can work together when it comes to saving, investing, or spending less. The hope is that with support (you know how I feel about accountability and support) you can get your friends on board and start to normalize these financial goals.

Here are some ideas:

- Biggest Saver. Create a game out of who can save the most money in a certain time period. It could be a week or a month, but cheer each other on and support one another throughout this challenge.

- Have a neighborhood yard or stoop sale. The family/person who has the most money at the end of the event wins an agreed-upon prize, in addition to bragging rights.

- When it comes to gift-giving, create a ceiling for gifts that *seems* low, say $10 or $25. You'll be amazed at what you come up with when you have to adhere to a certain limit

- Join in on a no-spend month. These are constantly happening online, but you can easily re-create it in person. Choose a month (February tends to be popular, as it's shorter) when you spend NOTHING outside of regularly scheduled expenses. Some people include a little wiggle room of $20 or so, but plenty of people make it through the month relatively unscathed.

- My gamify idea: _____

_____

_____

_____

_____

- My gamify idea: _____

_____

_____

_____

_____

- My gamify idea: _____

_____

_____

_____

_____

MONEY TALKS

One of my closest friends and I have been able to talk about money from day one. We met in high school and she was (and is) the kinda girl who is no BS. And that no BS translated to real talk about money. When it comes to money, nothing is off the table. We talk salaries, insecurities, hopes, and dreams. There is no awkwardness about choosing activities together or about who pays for what because we talk about it up-front, and if we aren't sure about something financially related, we ask. I know I got lucky with her. And I also realize how incredibly rare this is. Unless you, like me, hit the friend lottery and have someone to talk money with, it can be tough to find people you are comfortable talking with about money.

There aren't a ton of natural conversational openings where you can slip in something like, "And what's the ROI you're getting on that index fund?" or "How much did you pay for that new car?" without it feeling awkward. However, I know firsthand that most people are desperate to talk about money to other people. So many of my clients ask "Is this normal?" when it comes to their relationship with money. And my response probably kills them because there is no "normal" when it comes to money. But we are social creatures, and we like to gauge ourselves against our peers to see if we are on track.

A way to incorporate conversations about money without making anyone feel awkward is to create a money book club or mastermind in your community. I know of several money book clubs with topics like "Women and Wealth," "Couponing," and more. These groups meet monthly after having read an agreed-upon book. A money mastermind, on the other hand, is a bit more intimate as it serves as a space where you can talk about money in a format where you can get feedback, advice, and tips from others. A mastermind is typically a smaller group of people who have similar goals to bounce ideas off of one another, problem solve, and get feedback. These groups started in the business setting and were popularized by Napoleon

Hill, but I find they can work well in social settings. If you need help with the language, I've created a short email template for gauging their interest:

• WARM EMAIL •

"Hey you! I've noticed that at the last few neighborhood gatherings you seem pretty comfortable talking about your interest in Suze Orman. I'm starting to get serious about my retirement goals and wanted to reach out. I'm putting together a group of a few people to meet monthly and share ideas, tactics, and support around our financial goals. Is this something you'd be interested in?"

"Hey [NAME]! I've noticed that at [recent social gathering/meetup] you seem pretty comfortable talking about your interest in [financial guru/blogger or financial topic]. I'm starting to get serious about my [current financial] goals and wanted to reach out. I'm putting together a group of a few people to meet monthly and share ideas, tactics, and support around our financial goals. Is this something you'd be interested in?"

• COLD EMAIL •

"I am working on meeting a savings goal to take my family on vacation within the next 18 months. I notice we follow similar accounts, and I'm guessing we have similar goals. I'm interested in creating a face-to-face Mastermind of similarly minded people, where we can talk about financial tactics, ideas, and goals. Is this something you'd be interested in?"

"I am working on meeting a [financial goal] within the next [time frame]. I notice we follow similar accounts, and I'm guessing we have similar goals. I'm interested in creating a face-to-face Mastermind of similarly minded people, where we can talk about financial tactics, ideas, and goals. Is this something you'd be interested in?"

AWKWARD CONVERSATIONS

You have a list of alternative activities, a plan in place for spending quality time with friends that don't cost an arm and a leg, and you've even convinced a few friends to get on board. BUT (you knew there was a but) there are bound to be those times when you have to have what you feel are awkward money conversations with friends. A common financial anxiety distortion is imagining you know what others are thinking, or jumping to conclusions. These types of distortions tend to trip us up when it comes to interacting with others. Take a look at the example of how these cognitive distortions play out, and see if any of Jori's thoughts or behaviors look familiar.

Jori is excited to take a long weekend with his friends. They have all found a weekend that works—seriously one of the hardest parts these days—and the next phase of planning is finding somewhere to stay. A few hotels have been suggested that are pretty close to perfect. They are walking distance from Lake Michigan but close enough to town to be able to do land activities. The only problem is that they are pricier than what Jori had planned to spend. Sure, he could make it work, but he's really hoping to max out his Roth IRA, as security is a value to him. Taking this trip and spending a good chunk of money means it'll be that much harder for him to meet his values-based savings goal. He spends time finding other places they could stay but doesn't respond to the email chain because he doesn't want his friends to think he's cheap. He worries that they'll shoot down his idea or think that he isn't happy with the work they've done to find somewhere to stay. So he sits on it until he gets the email with the words, "Speak up now guys, I'm planning on booking after work today, unless there are any objections." In an anxiety-fueled moment, he quickly responds with the two Airbnb's he's found. Both of them have enough space for them to have their own room, there is parking, and while they are closer to town than the lake, they can still do a quick bike ride to make it. And …. shocker (no, not really) he gets an enthusiastic response from everyone, even the guy who had done the hotel research!

• CHALLENGE JUMPING TO CONCLUSIONS •

For the next few days, I want you to consciously track your thoughts when it comes to friends and money. Don't think they happen? You'd be surprised. The goal of this exercise is to help you first identify what your cognitive distortions are (remember those from Chapter 2?), and start challenging them by comparing the actual outcome to your assumed outcome. The idea behind this exercise is to start providing you/your brain with proof that more often than not, your worst social or financial fear doesn't come true.

SITUATION	ASSUMED OUTCOME	ACTUAL OUTCOME
Friends are about to book a pricey hotel for a long weekend. You feel it's out of your price range and search for more affordable Airbnbs	*They'll think I'm cheap. They'll think I don't appreciate the research they've done to find the hotels.*	*Friends were happy with the alternative lodging option.*

TEXTING TEMPLATES

Most of our awkward money conversations are in person, but let's be honest, much of our conversation is done via text, for better or for worse. I've included some easy texting templates you can use the next time you are struggling for words when it comes to friends and money.

SCENARIO	TEXTING RESPONSE
Your friend owes you money from dinner out a few weeks ago	*I almost forgot! I'm gonna shoot you a Venmo request for dinner at Osteria the other week.*
You get invited to a charity event that you can't afford right now	*I plan my charitable giving for the year and already earmarked my donations. Next time!*
You remember you owe your friend money to put toward the neighborhood fund	*It's been a while since you sent out the reminder, can you tell me what I owe you for our neighborhood fund?*

This chapter aimed to help you feel better about the relationship between your money and your social life. You can't avoid spending money altogether, nor should you, but I hope are getting more comfortable talking to your friends about money and feel like you have an arsenal of activities you can do to socialize that aren't so costly.

My top three takeaways from this chapter:

1. _____

2. _____

3. _____

CHAPTER 8

LOOKING FORWARD

"Making money and doing good in the world are not mutually exclusive."
—Arianna Huffington, author and founder of *The Huffington Post* and Thrive Global

You've done a lot of work focusing on your past and the present. Now we are going to look forward to help you start to create your financial future—and it's going to be FUN! We'll start by breaking down your goals into achievable steps, then find you a new money mantra, help you dream big, and help you think about how to plan for future financial changes.

SMART GOALS

Let's make your intention actionable now. Much has been said about SMART goals, and research backs up the importance of setting goals in that way. If you aren't sure of what a SMART goal is, it is Specific, Measurable, Attainable, Relevant, and Time-limited or Time-bound. We are going to take SMART goals to the next level by really breaking them down.

Among the many reasons we fail to achieve our goals is that we make our goals too big. You are going to make your goals small. And I mean super, super small. This isn't to patronize you or dissuade you from going after that big, hairy goal, it's to provide you with the momentum of achieving a small goal and the sense of accomplishment of having achieved it. Once you have one or two goals under your belt, it will fuel those bigger goals and boost your confidence to know you can achieve them.

Specific. What goal do you want to achieve? It's important, as I mentioned above, to really drill down on a particular item. Instead of "make more money," you want to say something like, "make an additional $350." If you are struggling to make a specific goal, sometimes it can be helpful to ask yourself more detailed questions such as: Why do I want to achieve this goal? Where? How?

Measurable. You need to be able to measure your goal. If you can't check it off of a list, it isn't measurable. It's important to measure your goal so you can track your progress and stay motivated. Additional questions you can ask yourself to drill down on measuring a goal include how many or how much?

Attainable. Is the goal going to be something you really can achieve? You don't want to set your goal too low, but if you overshoot your goal and miss it, you set yourself up for negative self-talk and discouragement. Think about the possible barriers to achieving your goal and preemptively problem-solve by getting them out of the way. If you regularly have four clients a month but have a few on a waitlist, it's pretty attainable to pick up an extra client or two.

Relevant. Does this goal matter to you? Is it worthwhile beyond just checking it off of a list?

Time-limited. Establish your target deadline. Having a deadline makes it more likely that you'll achieve your goal. Think about a project at work. If you know it's due on the fifteenth of the month, odds are that you get it done by the fifteenth. This, versus an ongoing project that tends to get put on the back burner for you to work on when you have extra time.

SMART Example

Specific. What goal do you want to achieve? "I will make an additional $1,000."

Measurable. "I will make an additional $1,000 by picking up one additional freelance project."

Attainable. I regularly have a waitlist of clients, meaning it will be easy for me to add on another to my workload. "I will make an additional $1,000 by picking up one additional freelance project by reaching out to a client on the waitlist."

Relevant. "I want to make an additional $1,000 so I can make an extra student loan payment and have extra fun money for next month's getaway."

Time-limited. "I want to make an additional $1,000 by the end of the month so I can make an extra student loan payment and have extra fun money for next month's getaway."

• SMART GOALS •

Choose ONE or TWO financial goals that you can and will achieve in one week and in one month.

S _____

M _____

A _____

R _____

T _____

S _____

M _____

A _____

R _____

T _____

INVEST IN FUTURE YOU

It's not uncommon to struggle thinking about setting goals five to ten or more years into the future. A 2011 Stanford study found that seeing your future self can actually help you implement behavioral changes in the present.[7] According to the study, seeing your future self makes your future-self more real and helps you to delay gratification now for the future rewards of having saved and invested money. This can help with everything from increasing your retirement contributions to exercising regularly for your future physical health. So grab your phone, snap a picture of your handsome self, and age it. There are several websites and a couple of

---

7   H. E. Hershfield, D. G. Goldstein, W. F. Sharpe, J. Fox, L. Yeykelis, L. Carstensen, and J. N. Bailenson. "Increasing Saving Behavior through Age-Progressed Renderings of the Future Self," *Journal of Marketing Research* 48 (2011): S23–S37.

apps that will do this. Save that picture, and put or paste it on the top of your Word doc with your life goals in it. Set it as your profile picture on your retirement account. Print it and put it on the top of your vision board. This is where you can use science to your advantage.

NEW MONEY MANTRA: GET RID OF MONEY BAGGAGE

I'm not frugal, or a budget queen, or a coupon-clipping person. While I love a good deal, I'm more interested in a well-rounded relationship with money. I struggle with two words: "budget" and "frugal." "Budget," because it feels punitive and restrictive. "Frugal," because it sounds like you are a miser. I prefer "spending plan" to the word "budget," and "intentional" or "mindful" over "frugal." These are small shifts that align with the practices I teach you in this book. The language we use when we talk to ourselves and sit down to plan for our financial futures *does* matter. Below is a list of affirmations you can use to create yourself a new money mantra. Feel free to tweak as needed. If these feel too tough, you can add the words "May I" or "May I someday" in front of the affirmations, as in "May I someday release all negative energy over money."

Affirmations

I am moving toward a debt-free life.

Each day I am more financially healthy.

Debt does not define me.

I can visualize what it will feel like to be debt-free.

I handle financial setbacks with courage.

I give thanks for the things money cannot buy.

Money comes to me in expected and unexpected ways.

I am worthy of making more money.

I am open and receptive to all the wealth life offers me.

I embrace new avenues of income.

I release all negative energy over money.

I deserve to be paid for my skills, time, and knowledge.

I can look at my finances without fear.

Money comes to me easily and effortlessly.

I use my money to better my life and the lives of others.

The fruits of my labors enrich the world, and I am rewarded generously.

My bills are paid on time and in full every month.

I am an excellent money manager.

Wealth constantly flows into my life.

My actions create constant prosperity.

I am aligned with the energy of abundance.

I constantly attract opportunities that create more money.

Money and spirituality coexist in harmony.

Money and love can be friends.

I am able to handle large sums of money.

I am at peace with having a lot of money.

I can handle success with grace.

Money expands my life's opportunities and experiences.

I control my money, my money does not control me.

Money creates a positive impact on my life.

I am capable of growth in my relationship with money.

My top three money affirmations:

1. _____

2. _____

3. _____

Remember those questions about your child-self and your future-self from Chapter 4?

Revisit them here:

How happy is your 5-year-old-self with your current life?

_____

_____

_____

_____

_____

How happy is your 85-year-old-self with your current life?

_____

_____

_____

_____

_____

DREAM BIG

In this section, I'll help you reverse-engineer your financial goals so you can see that those things you may have thought of as unachievable are likely doable. When you were learning how to set up your SMART goals, I said we'd start with teensy tiny goals to get some momentum going. Now, we'll use that momentum to dream big and help you create the life you'll love to live. And it's a simple question that I'll ask you: What financial goal do you want to achieve?

• MY BIG FINANCIAL GOALS •

Reverse engineering is when you look at an end result and break it down by working backward to figure out how you can achieve the result. When it comes to money, the beautiful thing is that all you need is a simple formula to figure out how much you need in order to achieve your goals. In this exercise, you'll see that some of those big dream-like financial goals might be closer than you'd previously thought. This exercise is helpful for all money personas, but especially for the Money Admirer. Since Money Admirers tend to think things would be better if there was more money, this exercise helps them see what exactly they want to use more money for. By creating a tangible goal, the Money Admirer can quantify what they are striving for.

Formulas

Annual: Divide goal by the number of years

Monthly: Divide goal by the number of months

Daily: Divide goal by the number of days

EXAMPLE: You want your business to bring in $275K of revenue over three years.

Annual: Divide goal by the number of years: $275,000/3=$91,666 each year

Monthly: Divide goal by the number of months: $275,000/36=$7,639 each month

Daily: Divide goal by the number of days $275,000/1,095=$251 each day

5-Year: What financial goal do you want to achieve in five years? How will you get there?

My Goal: _____

Annual goal: Divide by 5

Monthly goal: Divide by 60

Daily goal: Divide by 1,825

10-Year: What financial goal do you want to achieve in ten years? How will you get there?

My Goal: _____

Annual goal: Divide by 10

Monthly goal: Divide by 120

Daily goal: Divide by 3,650

15-Year: What financial goal do you want to achieve in fifteen years? How will you get there?

My Goal: _____

Annual goal: Divide by 15

Monthly goal: Divide by 180

Daily goal: Divide by 5,475

Which time frame felt best for me to see my financial goals—annual, monthly, or daily? What might be the reason for this?

_____

_____

_____

_____

What surprised me about seeing my financial goals in measurable, time-limited amounts?

_____

_____

_____

_____

PLAN FOR THE FUTURE

Here's a little bonus as you think about the goals you set for yourself: You are going to get pay raises and promotions along the way! This means it will be easier to save or invest in that goal, or that you'll be able to achieve your goal more quickly. In this section, we are going to plan ahead for things like raises and promotions, so you can really enjoy that extra money and not fall victim to lifestyle creep. Remember, lifestyle creep is when you start spending more money when you start earning more money. These are those small—or large—lifestyle upgrades we tell ourselves we deserve once we hit a financial milestone.

• STEPS TO AVOID LIFESTYLE CREEP •

Write Down Your Wants and Needs

Dream about and write out what you would do with an extra $2K, $5K, or $10K annually. Would you upgrade your washer and dryer? Put a bit more toward your credit card debt? Take that South American vacation? Or would it be nice to have a bit more fun money each month to not feel guilty about that annual sale at your favorite store? My guess is that this dream seems achievable if you had an additional chunk of money. Remind yourself of that vision if and when you get your next pay raise. Better yet, write it down in the notes section of your phone. I keep a Google doc of the things I want to purchase or use my money for that are currently out of reach. I reference it when I earn more money or get a tax refund. Now, it's your turn.

What I'd do with an additional:

$2,000 annually: _____

_____

$5,000 annually: _____

_____

$10,000 annually: _____

_____

$ _____ annually: _____

_____

• PLAN FOR RAISES AND/OR BONUSES •

You should be getting an annual raise that at least keeps pace with inflation. If not, take this as a sign to set up that meeting with your boss to talk about increasing your income, and plan for this raise. Most baseline raises are low, about 2.5% to 3%, as that more or less captures inflation. When you get that small inflation bump (going from $95K to $97,375K), pretend that you are still earning your former salary of $95K. Siphon off that additional increase in pay and reference the dream you'd written down above. See if you can do that thing. If there is additional money left over after funding that dream, throw extra money at your retirement or investment account. That's how you make a pay raise work for you.

When was the last time I had a pay raise?

_____

What is my anticipated inflation raise this upcoming year? How can I use it intentionally?

_____

_____

_____

_____

_____

Asking for a Raise

When you ask for a raise, be sure that you are prepared emotionally and with evidence. Before scheduling a meeting with your supervisor to ask for a raise, answer the following questions about yourself so you can be fully prepared:

- How long have I been with the company?

- What types of raises have I received?

- What types of responsibilities have I taken on since my last raise?

- What results have I brought to the company since my last raise (number of clients, money saved, revenue brought in, etc.)?

- What is the market rate for my position in my area?

When you ask for a raise, do not advocate that you need more money because you have more expenses. Your boss isn't interested in your personal finances; what they want to see is the value you bring to your position and to the company.

MIND YOUR TRIGGERS

We all have financial weak spots. Maybe your Achilles' heel is the "final sale" section at your favorite clothier's or the weekend getaway packages that land in your inbox. Plan a way that you can have your cake and eat it, too. Go back to that list of dream items. Does the flash sale get you closer to achieving that? If so, go for it! If not, hit pause and return to it later.

My financial Achilles' heels:

1. _____

2. _____

3. _____

Questions to ask when you feel an Achilles' heel purchase coming on:

Do I have money saved for this?

_____

Am I taking money away from a different values-based financial goal?

_____

Will I regret this in an hour? Will I regret it tomorrow?

_____

Even after answering the above questions, sometimes we just have to make things difficult. Gretchen Rubin applied long-known evidence in her book *Better Than Before*. In that book, she talked about how she put more obstacles between her and the "bad" habit. By doing this, it made it harder for her to "do" the bad habit. The more hoops you have to jump through to engage in that bad habit, the more likely it is that you'll give up before you get to it. Case in point, I know someone who is a self-described "shopaholic." Anytime she walks into a store, she walks out with something. So a quick run to pick up a prescription often meant she left with a handful of cosmetics, and picking up pants she'd had hemmed at the mall meant she'd buy a Cinnabon on the way out. She was getting much better at these unaccounted-for shopping sprees by consciously avoiding going into stores when she didn't have to. She started doing the drive-through for prescription pick-ups. She changed her dry cleaner to one that was a standalone instead of being inside a mall. When she went back-to-school shopping with her teenage sons, she only brought in the amount of cash she planned on spending for their supplies and clothes. This meant leaving her debit and credit cards at home.

Using your financial Achilles heels listed above, what hoops or barriers could you put in place to make it more difficult for you to fall off track?

FINANCIAL ACHILLES' HEEL	BARRIERS
Impulse Shopping	*Remove saved CC info from Amazon, sign up for prescription delivery instead of picking up meds from the pharmacy*

Working on your financial anxiety now can help prevent financial anxiety from popping up as intensely in the future. This chapter helped you find ways to think forward and plan without feeling overwhelmed.

My top three takeaways from this chapter:

1. _____

2. _____

3. _____

CHAPTER 9

ACCIDENTS HAPPEN

My goal in this chapter is to show you that you can make mistakes, embrace them, and learn from them. We will talk about how perfectionism can sabotage your financial growth, fostering resilience, and monitoring your readiness to change.

Thomas's story is a good place to start learning about how to be okay with setbacks or mistakes.

> After nine months of financial therapy work with Thomas, he verbalized that he was feeling terrible between sobs and blowing his nose. "But I don't get it!" he said. "I've been coming here, doing the exercises, and I'm still messing up!"

Thomas' would leave sessions feeling ready to take action, then return having implemented some but not all of the changes we'd discussed. He was beating himself up for not being able to make the changes he was hoping to make quickly enough.

As we explored his frustration, Thomas agreed that money isn't hard in a literal sense. He was an accountant, after all.

"So why am I still coming here?! How come I still get anxious?" he wondered.

I shared with him the reality of money. We interact with money in some way every day. We think about it. We work for it. We spend it. We exchange it. We lend it.

When it comes to a thing we use or interact with every day, it makes sense that it is going to take time to feel better about it. I shared with Thomas, like I've shared with many financial therapy clients, that if he'd sought a therapist for an eating disorder, he'd likely be in long-term treatment. Why? Because he'd have to interact with the thing causing him distress (food) daily. This is the same with money. There isn't a quick fix. This is a process, a series of exercises, a method that takes time in order to feel okay in our personal financial relationship.

By normalizing the reality of money and behavior change, Thomas was able to be more compassionate toward himself. He kept coming to therapy and was able to see each change implemented as a victory, instead of wanting to see all the changes happen immediately.

My hope is that you'll use Thomas' story to keep you going on your journey to a healthy financial relationship. Many of us are sold on the idea that we have to be perfect, or damn near perfect, in order to be considered successful.

EMBRACING FAILURE

Financial gurus and successful entrepreneurs have all experienced financial failure. Author, radio host, and businessman Dave Ramsey declared bankruptcy. Financial advisor, author, and television host Suze Orman lost her first investors' $50K through a poor investment. Fashion designer Rebecca Minkoff spent $10K on fabric before she had any orders. Personal trainer and television personality Jillian Michaels was reportedly intimidated by money, so she hired someone who ended up making a mistake that caused her to double-pay her taxes. Mistakes happen and the best thing we can do is embrace them and learn from them.

One thing I've noticed when I'm working with clients is once they start to get on a roll in their progress, they also start to trend toward perfectionism. There are many definitions of perfectionism floating around. I've grabbed a few of my favorites to share here:

"A disposition to regard anything short of perfection a failure"
—Merriam-Webster

"People whose standards are beyond reach or reason"
—Dr. David Burns

"People who strain compulsively and unremittingly toward impossible goals and who measure their own worth entirely in terms of productivity and accomplishment"
—Dr. David Burns

While all of those are technically right, here's the one that I agree with most fully.

Perfectionism is "an attempt to control your emotions and decrease discomfort."[8]

Sure, you may be afraid of failure or be guilty of overshooting your standard, but what's behind that? It's a feeling of discomfort. Of feeling anxious. Of feeling disheartened. Of feeling humiliated. And rather than feel temporarily uncomfortable, we try desperately to control situations, leading to perfectionism. Even if you don't consider yourself a perfectionist, I encourage you to read and follow along with this chapter. For most of us, perfectionism shows up in certain areas, and when it comes to our money, we have to be okay making mistakes along the way.

Yes, I did just say you have to be okay making financial mistakes.

So where do we get this drive to be perfect? Some studies suggest genetic influences, others point to learned behavior. In this book, we'll be focusing on learned behaviors as there isn't much we can do about genetic predisposition.

LEARNED BEHAVIORS

We learn to fear failure through many external cues, and they become a learned behavior. These can start when we are very young, and the lessons about fearing failure often continue to show up throughout our lives. We fear getting sent to time out (failure), getting a bad grade (failure), not being invited to a sleepover (failure), being dumped (failure), not making varsity (failure), and on and on. We learn that these "failures" are bad, feel bad, and should be avoided at all costs.

Let's first start with nonfinancial examples of learned behaviors and how they may cause us to fear failure.

---

8   M. M. Antony and R. P. Swinson, *When Perfect Isn't Good Enough: Strategies for Coping with Perfectionism.* (Berkeley, CA: New Harbinger Publications, 2009.)

● LEARNED FEAR OF FAILURE ●

In this exercise, you'll learn the four main ways the fear of failure is reinforced: reward, punishment, modeling, and instruction. You'll get an example or two in each category, then you will reflect on times when you picked up these various reinforcements along the way.

TYPE OF REINFORCEMENT	EXAMPLE	MY EXAMPLE OF REINFORCEMENT
Reward: Receiving a positive cue or signal for a behavior	"I studied longer than others in high school and got good grades," or "Watching my carb intake helped me feel better in my clothes."	
Punishment: Receiving a negative consequence following a behavior	"I got in trouble when I didn't put my laundry away," or "I got made fun of for stuttering."	
Modeling: Learning to behave in a certain way by observing others	"My dad couldn't relax until everything from dinner was cleaned up," or "My favorite coach had a regimen she swore was what made her successful."	
Instruction: Learning from the media, other people, or other information sources	"My whole life I was told that medicine was my best career choice," or "There are so many more likes on my Instagram when I post a flattering photo."	

•FINANCIAL REINFORCEMENT•

Now that you have an idea of where lessons are picked up along the way, this exercise encourages you to drill into the financial lessons you may have internalized. As in the previous exercise, I'll give you examples of how these may look to help you get started.

TYPE OF REINFORCEMENT	EXAMPLE	MY EXAMPLE OF REINFORCEMENT
Reward: Receiving a positive cue or signal for a behavior	"Working longer hours means I get overtime and more money," or "My dad would always give me a wink when I was able to donate some of my babysitting money into the offering plate at church."	
Punishment: Receiving a negative consequence following a behavior	"When I tried to ask my mom about money when I was a kid, I was told that it is 'rude' to talk about money," or "I asked my husband about money early in our relationship and was told that his debt was his business."	
Modeling: Learning to behave in a certain way by observing others	"A neighbor who looks financially successful gets a new car every 18 to 24 months," or "My aunt would freak out if she misplaced her coupon organizer."	
Instruction: Learning from the media, other people, or other information sources	"If you go into a career you love, it shouldn't be about the money," or "Dave Ramsey says all debt is bad debt, and he's really popular!"	

What did you learn about the reinforcement you received about money?

_____

_____

_____

_____

Were there any areas that surprised you?

_____

_____

_____

_____

PERFECTION AND FAILURE

Many of us think negatively of failure. In this section, I'll highlight what science (and some creatives) have found about the growth potential of failing. Failing can lead to change, build resilience, create "a-ha" moments, be humbling, and enhance growth potential. Let's talk about how.

Many clients give up trying to take control of their money because they make a mistake, feel overwhelmed, then toss their whole plan out the window. This is akin to a person who sets a goal of running a 10K by the end of the month after years of no consistent exercise. On their first week of training, they jump into running a 5K, then an 8K. Their hamstrings and calves are sore, feet blistered, and parts of their body chafed that they didn't know was possible, so they decide that they aren't a runner and resign to never run again.

You HAVE to give yourself permission to take things slowly and not aim to be perfect. You will mess up. You will make mistakes. AND, you'll be fine. You'll be able to keep going on your journey to eliminating your financial anxiety.

• ◼ MANTRAS FOR STRIVING ◼ •

Review the following list of statements aimed to help you feel better with "failure" or imperfection. Jot down the ones that resonate and keep them on you. Some of my clients have used sticky notes, where others prefer to use a notes app on their phone.

- Done is better than perfect (Sheryl Sandberg)

- Good enough

- Move fast and break things

- I have the courage to be imperfect

- I can enjoy the journey and steps along the way

- Perfection is an illusion

- Nature doesn't wait for perfection

- Perfect is the enemy of good (Voltaire)

- Done creates results and momentum

- I can tolerate uncertainty

- Everything is "figureoutable" (Marie Forleo)

- I can tweak something after I've made a decision

- I'm humble enough to accept constructive criticism

MOTIVATIONAL INTERVIEWING

Motivational Interviewing was created to help people who were recovering from addictive substances by getting them on board with creating and making behavioral changes rather than forcing change upon them. This created a dynamic where both the expert and the client were collaborating on the change. The MI researchers found that by having the client identify why it was important they change, they were more likely to make healthy behavior changes.

Let me illustrate with an example:

> Tessa, a Blissfully Ignorant, wasn't feeling great. It was the end of yet another pay period and her retirement contribution still sat at $0. She knew she needed to start putting money toward retirement, but something almost always came up that prevented her from feeling like she was able. Last month, she needed a new water heater, and the month before, she forgot that she needed to board her dog for a week-long business trip. She just felt like there wasn't anything extra. Feeling discouraged, she sent an email to her HR rep asking for the contact information for their retirement advisor. Each employee got one free retirement advising appointment per year.

At the advising appointment, she came away feeling even worse. The advisor had said not only did she have to start saving yesterday, to even be close to being on track for retirement, she'd have to max out her retirement for at least six years. "You are so far behind. You should have made this appointment and started saving years ago."

This type of response is typical of a person in an "expert" position; they advise and prescribe but don't do a good job of getting the individual they are working with on board for the reasons it might be important for them to make a change. I'm sure you can think of a personal experience when an expert told you what to do.

Let's imagine that Tessa's retirement advising appointment had gone differently. Instead of the expert prescriptive advice, the retirement advisor had taken a Motivational Interviewing seminar. The exchange, instead of being one-sided, went like this:

Advisor, "I see you are ready to start saving for retirement. That's great! What makes you feel like now is a good time to get started?"

Tessa, "Well, I know I should have started a while ago, but this was the first month I didn't have any financial hiccups so I thought I'd get going now."

Advisor, "You had a month where things were going well financially and are ready to take the next steps. You probably know you have some catching up to do, is it okay to talk about some options?"

Tessa, "Yeah, I know I'm behind, but I'd like to hear the different options."

Advisor, "Okay, well, you could go all in this year and put as much as possible toward your retirement, but that would likely mean you'd have to stop all extra spending and cut from your budget. You could also try a tiered approach. With lots of clients, we start with 1 to 2% going toward their retirement and automatically increasing it each month by a percent until we hit 10%. Or, you can start with 5% and keep it at that contribution level for a while. Do any of those sound good to you?"

Tessa, "I like the idea of slowly increasing it. Can you tell me more about the automation process?"

In this exchange, the advisor sits back a bit more. Tessa and the advisor know she's behind; rather than forcing Tessa to listen and overwhelming her, the advisor took an approach that allowed Tessa to choose what worked best for her situation.

The power behind Motivational Interviewing is that it allows the person who is considering making a behavior change to really tap into what makes it important to make a change. Instead of someone else telling you what to do, you get the opportunity to see what works best for you and create a more sustainable plan.

• WHAT IS YOUR MOTIVATION TO CHANGE? •

If you've had a few hiccups along the way as you've worked through this book, now is a good time to check in and remind yourself why you wanted to stop financial anxiety in the first place. Spend some time answering the following questions to reconnect to your "why."

Why did I originally pick up this book?

_____

_____

_____

_____

_____

What has made it hard to finish the exercises?

_____

_____

_____

_____

Which exercises have been the most rewarding? Why do I think that is?

_____

_____

_____

_____

What has made it challenging to implement some financial anxiety strategies?

_____

_____

_____

_____

_____

What would life be like if I made these changes?

_____

_____

_____

_____

_____

What happens if things stay the same?

_____

_____

_____

_____

_____

When I've had setbacks in the past, how have I persevered?

_____

_____

_____

_____

STAGES OF CHANGE

Stages of Change are another part of Motivational Interviewing. The idea is that as a person implements behavioral changes, they go through a series of stages of readiness to change. As you go through them, you'll be able to see which stage of readiness you are in when it comes to making financial behavioral changes.

I'll include examples of potential behavior with Keith as we go through this model.

> Keith, a self-identified Spender, has been hiding his spending from his partner Liz for a long time. He thinks spending on little things that she'd get upset about isn't worth telling her because it'd just cause an argument. They've talked about hiding spending from one another in the past, and it got so heated that they have avoided talking about it for almost two years. Keith works around the corner from a local food market. He loves that there are over 20 options for food and has fun trying new foods with his coworkers at lunch and his friends after work. He usually ends up eating at the market four to five times per week, unbeknownst to Liz.

1. Precontemplation. In this stage, people do not intend to take action in the foreseeable future (defined as within the next six months). People are often unaware that their behavior is problematic or produces negative consequences. People in this stage often underestimate the pros of changing behavior and place too much emphasis on the cons of changing behavior. *Keith thinks that telling Liz is stupid. It'd just make her mad and really isn't any of her business. He's not interested in telling her or stopping his spending.*

2. Contemplation. In this stage, people intend to start the healthy behavior within the next few months. They recognize that their behavior may be problematic, and take more thoughtful and practical consideration of the pros and cons of changing the behavior, with an equal emphasis placed on both. Even with this recognition, people may still feel ambivalent toward changing their behavior. *Keith almost "got caught" eating at the market. He had a day when he'd ended up coming home with take-out, not knowing Liz would be there. When she spotted his carryout bag, he quickly lied that his boss had taken the office out for meeting their sales goals that quarter. After the exchange, he started to think about his behavior. On the one hand, he knew if Liz found out, there'd be an argument, and on the other hand, it was such a part of his routine and also a great way to get out of the office*

3. Preparation. In this stage, people are ready to take action within the next month. They start to take small steps toward behavioral change, and they believe changing their behavior can lead to a healthier life. *Keith read an article about how millennials spend an average of $3,000 more annually on take-out than baby boomers. This number stopped him in his tracks because he realized he and Liz had been talking about taking a week off to go camping in Yosemite but haven't been able to save the cash. He starts to recognize that cutting back on his love of the food market would mean they could take that trip together sooner. He tells himself that starting next week, on April 1, he'll cut back.*

4. Action. In this stage, people have recently changed their behavior and intend to keep moving forward with that behavioral change. They may exhibit this by modifying their problem behavior or acquiring new healthy behaviors. *Keith has cut back on his food market habit a ton! In the past month, he's only visited the market three times! Not only has it felt good to see the money in the vacation fund start to creep up, he notices he feels less edgy when he and Liz go out to eat because he doesn't feel like he's been hiding his take-out habits from her.*

5. Relapse. This stage is still debated among therapists and researchers. Some feel it isn't okay to include this in the stages because it sets people up to fall into old habits. I'm including it because it says IT'S ALL RIGHT to make mistakes. Change might happen on the first or tenth try. I believe you can keep going and this stage tells you that you aren't alone and still have the steps in place to make the change moving forward. *After a rough week at work, Keith finds himself sitting at the stool of his favorite tapas vendor three days in a row.*

6. Maintenance. In this stage, people have sustained their behavioral change for three months or more and intend to maintain the behavioral change going forward. People in this stage work to prevent relapse to earlier stages. *Nearing the end of September, Keith has made and adhered to a rule of only eating out once a week (yay for beating decision fatigue!). He told*

Liz about his previous takeout habit last month and together they worked out a way for them to have a bit more discretionary spending so neither one felt deprived.

● THINK ABOUT YOUR STAGE OF CHANGE ●

Think about the financial habit you are trying to change. Write it here:

_____

Based on the above six stages of readiness to change, which stage of change are you in when you think about the financial habit you are trying to change?

_____

If you are in any stage besides maintenance, consider how motivating it is to you to make the change on a scale of 1 to 10 with 1 being not motivated at all and 10 being extremely motivated.

_____

If you ranked yourself at anything aside from a 10, what would help you get to a higher number?

_____

FOSTERING RESILIENCE

Let's talk about the importance of regimen. Remember in Chapter 2 when we reviewed decision fatigue? Having a structured, predictable day helps to quiet anxiety and reduce decision fatigue. Plus, once your day is structured and predictable, the things that inevitably pop up that aren't predictable are less impactful.

Sample Daily Regimen Log

TIME OF DAY	TASK	FINANCIAL TASK
6 a.m.	Wake up and exercise	
7 a.m.	Shower and get ready for work, leave for work	Check budgeting app
8 a.m.	Arrive at work	
Noon	Lunch break	
1 to 5 p.m.	Finish work	
6 p.m.	Arrive home, do chores	
7 p.m.	Eat dinner	
8 p.m.	Take dog for a walk	
9 p.m.	Watch TV/Read	
11 p.m.	Go to bed	Practice a grounding exercise

Now it's time to create your daily regimen log by completing the chart below:

TIME OF DAY	TASK	FINANCIAL TASK
6 a.m.		
7 a.m.		
8 a.m.		
Noon		
1 to 5 p.m.		
6 p.m.		
7 p.m.		
8 p.m.		
9 p.m.		
11 p.m.		

Finally, keep in mind that behavioral change takes time. I know I've said this in various ways up until now, but one of the best metaphors for this is boiling a pot of water. Even when the burner is on high and the pot is on the stove, it still takes time for the water to heat up. That is to say, even when you have your finances on autopilot, you are practicing healthy money mantras and are insightful about your stage of behavioral change, it's still going to take some time for your mind to catch up to your changes. Practice compassion and kindness while you charter this new financial territory.

My top three takeaways from this chapter:

1. _____

2. _____

3. _____

CONCLUSION

You've made it! You've internalized, or at least started to open your mind, to the fact that money isn't a dirty word. You are fully on the path to creating a healthy, non-anxious relationship with money.

Remember my money story that I shared at the beginning of this book? It included things like, "I believe that if you are born into a life of privilege, you should give back to your community," "Money is a tool that can provide peace of mind and happiness," And "Money isn't the only thing that is important in life, but having it helps to free up mental energy to spend on other things in life."

It took me time, energy, patience, and lots of repetition to get to this point. It's important that as you continue to work on your financial anxiety, you give yourself permission to be flexible. There may be certain exercises in the book that are worth repeating a few times. There could be certain chapters that feel particularly tough. Check in and ask yourself why. What was it about the chapters that felt really good; why were the exercises fun to complete? Check back in with why those chapters resonated.

Let's quickly review what you've learned. You've learned your money story and where your relationship with money came from. You've learned what anxiety is, how to notice it, and how to address it. You've got the basics of personal finance down, from budgeting to retirement. You've connected with your values and learned how to apply your values to your personal finances so you feel good about the way you are saving, spending, and investing. You've learned ways to implement new healthy coping skills to quiet your mind and body when financial anxiety comes up. You've learned ways to connect with friends that involve activities besides spending money. You've created a tangible financial goal for your future and learned ways to handle setbacks with grace.

Are you ready for the final exercise in this book? You are going to end with where you began.

What is my relationship with money like?

_____

_____

_____

_____

What is my money doing for me?

_____

_____

_____

_____

What is my money doing for others; for my community?

_____

_____

_____

_____

Congratulations! You've taken the time to explore your relationship with money and learned ways to fight your financial anxiety!

For more guidance, visit my website www.mindmoneybalance.com. I'm also on YouTube @Lindsaybryanpodvin, Instagram @mindmoneybalance, and Facebook @mindmoneybalance.

NOTES

RESOURCES

Books

Broke Millennial: Stop Scraping By and Get Your Financial Life Together by Erin Lowry

Smart Couples Finish Rich by David Bach

Smart Women Finish Rich by David Bach

The Art of Money by Bari Tessler

Your Money or Your Life: 9 Steps to Transforming Your Relationship with Money and Achieving Financial Independence by Vicki Robin

Podcasts

So Money with Farnoosh Torabi

Bad with Money with Gaby Dunn

Trailblazers 2050 with Rianka Dorsainvil

Beyond the Dollar with Sara Li-Cain

BIBLIOGRAPHY

Antony, M. M. and R. P. Swinson. *When Perfect Isn't Good Enough: Strategies for Coping with Perfectionism.* Berkeley, CA: New Harbinger Publications, 2009.

Danziger, S., J. Levav, and L. Avnaim-Pesso. "Extraneous Factors in Judicial Decisions." *Proceedings of the National Academy of Sciences* 108 no. 17 (2011): 6889–92.

Hershfield, H. E., D. Goldstein, W. F. Sharpe, J. Fox, L. Yeykelis, L. Carstensen, and J. N. Bailenson. "Increasing Saving Behavior through Age-Progressed Renderings of the Future Self. *Journal of Marketing Research* 48 (2011): S23–S37. doi: 10.1509/jmkr.48.SPL.S23.

Kinder, G., and M. Rowland. *Life Planning for You: How to Design and Deliver the Life of Your Dreams.* Littleton, MA: Serentiy Point Press, 2014.

Lawson, D., B. Klontz, and S. L. Britt. "Money Scripts." In *Financial Therapy*, edited by B. Klontz, S. L. Britt, and K. L. Archuleta, 23–24. New York: Springer, 2015).

Ma, X., Z. Q. Yue, Z. Q. Gong, H. Zhang, N. Y. Duan, Y.T. Shi, G. Wei, and Y.F. Li. "The Effect of Diaphragmatic Breathing on Attention, Negative Affect and Stress in Healthy Adults." *Frontiers in Psychology* 8 no. 874 (2017). doi:10.3389/fpsyg.2017.00874.

Mellan, O., S. Christie, J. Bodnar, and P. McMoon. *Money Harmony: A Road Map for Individuals and Couples.* Washington, DC: Money Harmony Books, 2014.

Speece, M. W. and S. B. Brent. "Children's Understanding of Death: A Review of Three Components of a Death Concept." *Child Development* 55, no. 5 (1984): 1671–86.

ACKNOWLEDGMENTS

"Writing a book" hadn't been on my to-do list. When Bridget from Ulysses Press reached out to inquire about my willingness to take on this project, I had to google and pinch myself to be sure this wasn't an error. Over a year, I've learned so much about what goes into articulating spastic thoughts and getting them out on paper. This book couldn't have been done without the support of so many around me.

The deepest of thanks to my partner Ray for knowing I could knock out a book in five months and casually said, "You'll do it in less." Thank you for your love, humor, and steadfastness. I love you more than you know. In our wedding vows, we exchanged, "I love you for who you are now, and who you are yet to be." Thank you for letting me add "author" to that expansive, open role of "who you are yet to be."

To my family. Thank you to my in-laws Eileen and Tim, who regularly shared their pride and checked in on my well-being and progress during the writing process. My siblings, including Colleen, Aryana, Bryana, Mysha, Stephanie, Jessica, and Ryan, for the constant encouragement and sharing in my excitement. To my mom, who never doubted my capabilities. Thank you.

To all those at Grove Emotional Health Collaborative who understood my being a recluse on Mondays by providing physical and emotional space for me to write. 92% of this book was written in the office of 214 S. Main Street.

To the women of my bi-monthly Mastermind: Monica, Ida, Julie, and Lauren. Thank you for holding space for me to air my fears, worries, and joys.

To my dearest money friend Alisha, I've won the friendship lotto with you, and I don't ever forget it (referenced on page 116).

To my former boss Anne, who taught me how to get comfortable building a plane as it's flown.

And to my editor, Bridget Thoreson, for seeking me out and cheering me on. Without you, this book would not exist.

ABOUT THE AUTHOR

Lindsay Bryan-Podvin is an author, financial therapist, and speaker who started her career in the field of mental health treatment and advocacy. As the first financial therapist in Michigan, she combines financial literacy with the emotional and psychological side of money. She always had an interest in mental health and found an even greater love working at the intersection of mental health and wealth. It's her mission to open up a dialogue to talk about money beyond the dollars and cents. She has a degree in sociology from Michigan State University and a master's degree in social work from the University of Michigan. She lives with her husband, and Portuguese water dog, in Ann Arbor, Michigan. You can find Lindsay online at www.mindmoneybalance.com or on Instagram @mindmoneybalance.